Mission: Imponderable

Darren Bane was born at a very early age and has persistently refused to grow up ever since. While some are born with a silver spoon in their mouths, he believes he was born with a plastic picnic fork in his backside and has subsequently stumbled through life living under the cloud of the Sadim Touch, which is the opposite of the Midas Touch. Nevertheless, he has fought off the apparently inevitable mental breakdown by practicing the philosophy that laughter is the best medicine and that it is something that is enjoyed all the more when shared, which he hopes to do through the publication of this nonsensical book.

Mission: Imponderable

Darren Bane

2019

First published in 2019

ISBN: 978-0-244-18911-2

db07

Published by db books
www.darrenbane.co.uk

Printed and distributed using the self-publishing platform Lulu
www.lulu.com

Contents

Introduction

"Your mission, should you choose to accept it...", well, actually, this has been more of a calling than a mission.

When I was growing up (although some would suggest that this is still very much a work in progress and that I've still got some considerable way to go), one of my favourite comedians was Jasper Carrott.

In 1982, he released an album (there were few stand-up comedy repeats on TV back then, far fewer channels, no YouTube clips, no digital downloads or 'catch-up' TV options, and not very many video recorders either, so an album was the easiest way of catching a repeat performance of favourite comedy moments) called *The Best of the Chat from Carrott's Lib,* a collection of monologues from his Saturday evening TV show, which I was an avid viewer of.

In a track called Black Box, he queries why aircraft weren't constructed from the same material as the black box flight recorders, since whenever there was a tragic incident, pretty much the only thing that almost always survived intact was the black box. (Let's ignore the fact that these black boxes are orange – that's *another* question!). He suggested that if planes were constructed from the same material then should an aircraft crash into a mountain, all you are likely to lose is the mountain.

It made sense, in a funny kind of way, I thought. And thus, I had my introduction to the world of the imponderable question.

I soon became aware of several other seemingly well-established imponderables, such as "how do snow plough drivers get to work on the morning of a blizzard?" and "how do kitchenware manufacturers get the Teflon non-stick coating to stick to the inside of their frying pans?"

Because such musings tickled my own funny bone, I made it my 'Mission Imponderable' to write them down as and when I discovered them, and that's what I've done since 1982.

As I aged chronologically (as opposed to grew up), many such dilemmas would arise during alcohol-fuelled nonsensical discussions in bars among friends, which I would quickly write down; I would overhear others in conversations in the workplace or when out and about.

The dawn of the digital age saw several websites include sections on imponderables, which I would occasionally dedicate some specific time to seeking out, and I also came up with some original ones of my own.

There were some very common questions that arose repeatedly – like the aforementioned 'snow plough driver' and 'non-stick frying pan coating' ones – which I came to consider as 'classics', together with plenty of one-offs, in addition to my own creations.

So, what exactly *is* an imponderable question? Strictly speaking, the term 'imponderable' describes a situation that isn't able to be completely explained or that defies our ability to comprehend.

If something is ponderable, it *can* be assessed or weighed. Therefore, imponderable is something that is elusive and vague. An imponderable question is one which does not have a definitive answer, a clear yes or no, right or wrong; it's more of a grey area than a clear black and white, a chicken and egg situation, you might say.

The asking of such imponderable questions is sometimes a little genuinely thought provoking, often humorous, and frequently downright daft. During many a wibbling discussion in the pub, someone has posed an imponderable and said something along the lines of, "there you go, that's something for you to think about, and to keep you awake at night."

Such a sentiment served to add something of a deeper meaning to my mission, as I realised – being someone who frequently struggled to sleep soundly myself – that what I had was, potentially, the perfect publication for insomniacs; in fact, I'd go so far as to claim it is an insomniac's dream.

Can insomniac's dream? Well, that's yet another imponderable...

What I mean is that, for those who spend restless nights tossing and turning in tired torment, here is a book of bite-size snippets that you could dip in and out of to help pass some of the time while persistently failing in your quest to find the land of nod.

It may even spread the odd smile or two and help relieve the tension of your tirelessly torturous nights.

Since an insomniac's nights are often long and lonely, the book also serves another useful purpose as, for those who have absolutely no difficult whatsoever in slipping into a very deep sleep the split second their heads hit their pillows, there is sure to be a question of two in here that will undoubtedly keep them awake at night too, and thus they can keep their insomniac companions company and both have something to talk about into the bargain.

So, I sorted through my scattered scribblings, arranged the imponderables into something resembling coherent categories, and this book is the result.

I wouldn't dare suggest that this compilation is, in any way, a complete collection of imponderables, but I think I *can* claim that it is quite comprehensive, although I'm sure many of you will soon find yourselves coming up with imponderables of your own, as I did.

Should you not be an insomniac, and also not want your sleep disturbed, I think you'll find it is also the perfect bathroom book. Not because it's full of crap, but again because it has nice little nuggets, if you will, that you can randomly browse through to pass the time.

Ultimately, as long as there is something within these pages that forces you into a grin (albeit a somewhat tired, forced effort, perhaps more of a grimace) at least once, then I, for one, *will* sleep soundly, with the satisfaction of knowing that this is now a case of Mission Accomplished.

Enjoy.

DB, June 2019

Animal Crackers

What are male ladybirds called?

What's the proper name for a female Daddy Long Legs?

Do jellyfish come in different flavours?

Why don't sheep shrink during torrential rainfall?

Do hedgehogs ever suffer from prickly heat?

If a fly loses its wings, should it be called a walk? And do you call a dog without a bone 'floppy'?

If flies are called flies because they fly, why aren't fish called swims?

Do rabbits consider their own feet to be lucky? And if you have a 'lucky' rabbits' foot as a charm, what happened to the rabbit that the foot came from.

If a glo-worm backed into a fan, would it be de-lighted?

Do earwigs have ears and, if so, can they 'wig' or wiggle them?

What do restless ants get in their pants?

If a man sees a ring of little tweety birds dancing around his head after he has banged it, what to little tweety birds see?

Do turtles wear people-necked sweaters?

Do ants sneeze?

Do fish console their lovesick friends by reminding them that there are plenty more girls on the land?

If birdwatching is called ornithology, why don't twitchers refer to the subject of their attention as "orniths"?

Do animals bark/growl/squeak with different accents, and in different languages?

If man evolved from monkeys and apes, why do we still have monkeys and apes?

If rhino horn is meant to be such an effective aphrodisiac, why are rhino's endangered species? And how on earth did anyone discover that rhino horn is an aphrodisiac in the first place?

If a cow laughed really hard, would milk come out of its nose?

Do one-legged ducks swim in circles?

Do sheep get static cling if they rub up against one another?

If moths find light so attractive, why don't they come out during the day, when they could have as much light as they could possibly desire?

If cows prefer to drink water rather than milk, do they know something that we don't?

If you put a chameleon in a room full of mirrors, what colour would it turn?

Is there a website for spiders?

Is a donkey with three legs called a wonkey?

Does a badly-behaved horse come from an unstable environment?

Have any hummingbirds ever learned the words to any songs?

If you put a chicken into a shell suit, would you call it an egg?

If two silkworms finished simultaneously in a race, would it be said that they had tied?

If the early bird gets the worm, why is it that it's the second mouse which gets the cheese?

What do you do if you see an endangered species earing an endangered plant?

If a tortoise doesn't have a shell, is it homeless or naked?

If a pig loses its voice, does it become disgruntled? Or is this the correct term for a castrated pig?

Do fish get thirsty?

If cats and dogs didn't have fur, would we still pet them?

Has anyone ever seen a toad sitting on a toadstool?

What do sheep count when they can't get to sleep?

After eating, are amphibians advised to wait an hour before getting out of the water?

Do butterflies remember the days when they were caterpillars?

Are all pigeons pigeon-toed, or if a pigeon's feet point inwards, is it considered to be human-toed?

Why don't woodpeckers get headaches?

Do crabs think we all walk sideways?

If you crossed a terrier with a bulldog, would the result be terribull? Can you really cross a bulldog with a shih tzu, or is it just bull...?

Why do we wait until a pig is dead before curing it? Isn't that a case of too little, too late?

What's so special about bee's knees?

Do a mating pair of boa constrictors have a crush on each other?

If they are supposed to be extinct, why are there so many mammoth sales?

If cattle have a sense of humour, are they considered to be a laughing stock?

Do micro-organisms eat microchips?

If it's a 'dog eat dog' world, why are there still so many dogs?

Which was the first cat to persuade its owner to install a cat flap?

Why don't bulldog clips look remotely anything like a bulldog?

Why is the height of a horse measured in 'hands', when tradition dictates that 'feet' is the more commonly-used unit of measurement? Although how on earth did *that* come about?

Do birds get tickled by their feathers?

Are zebras white with black stripes or black with white stripes?

Why do they call it "getting your dog fixed" when, after the procedure, certain bits don't work anymore?

If a dog sweats through its tongue, why does it have armpits?

Does a cold goose get people bumps?

Why are rubber duckies most commonly yellow, when real ducks aren't?

Does chocolate milk come from brown cows?

Does a man-eating shark discriminate, or does it also eat women, too?

If you fed a bee nothing but oranges, would it start making marmalade?

Do flies on walls ever really notice everything that is going on?

If you put some birdseed into soil and watered it, would you be able to grow a bird?

Where did house spiders live, and what were they called, before humans started building homes?

How do they persuade ducks, deer etc to cross at the animal crossing signs?

Why aren't greyhounds grey?

If you throw a young cat out of a car window, does it become kitty litter?

Why hasn't evolution allowed bees to stop dying as soon as they use their sting, or allow flies and wasps to learn how to sniff out fresh air so that they can fly out of the chasm-like gap in the window that you have just opened for them, rather than continue to buzz up and down against the glass aimlessly?

Are guide people provided for blind dogs?

Why do dogs go mad if you blow in their face, but when you take them out in the car, they stick their heads out of the window?

What happens when none of your bees wax?

Why don't you ever see any baby pigeons?

When pigeons walk, their heads bob up and down really fast. Doesn't that give them a really bad headache?

Can a pig pull a hamstring?

How is it that a bird can fly but a fly can't bird?

Do hungry crows have ravenous appetites?

When vultures are about to die, do they ever get tempted to start eating themselves?

How can they tell that twin lobsters really *are* twins?

Why do dogs insist on sniffing each others' backsides to say hello? Why don't they just bark in their face or something?

Do fish sleep?

Does anyone actually kill two birds with one stone?

Why do birds have white poop?

When a fly lands on the ceiling, at what point does it turn upside down?

Do bees get wax in their ears?

If a dog's sense of smell is 100 times greater than that of a human, why do dogs insist on sticking their noses up the butt of other dogs or even people?

If we can't air, does that mean that fish can't see water?

If Mynah birds can talk, why do you never hear two of them having a conversation?

If you have a pet with two heads, do you have to name both heads?

Do cows have calf muscles? (Is this what they used when they give birth?)

How do dead bugs end up inside those enclosed light fixtures?

Is a distorted tortoise simply called an oise?

If cockroaches can survive atomic bombs and nuclear warfare, what on earth is inside a can of Raid?

Classic Conundrums

How does a snow plough driver get to work in the morning after a severe blizzard the night before?

How do the manufacturers of kitchenware get the Teflon non-stick coating to adhere to the surface of their frying pans?

Why aren't aircraft made out of the same material that black boxes are made out of? And why are black boxes called black boxes, when most of them are orange?

Why doesn't cat food come in Mouse Flavour, and dog food come in Cat Flavour?

Why are wrong telephone numbers never engaged?

How do the 'keep off the grass' signs get onto the grass? Similarly, how do the 'thin ice' signs get safely put onto the thin ice?

How can you tell if your pen has run out of invisible ink?

Why do magazines feel the need to promote the offer of *free* gifts? Aren't all gifts free?

Why is it that is someone tells you there are one billion stars in the universe, you believe the, but if they warn you that the paint on the door is wet, you still have to touch it?

What is an occasional table the rest of the time?

Why is it that when a door is left open, it's ajar, but when you leave a jar of something open, it's never referred to as adoor?

Why is there only one Monopolies and Mergers Commission?

If the No.2 pencil is so popular, why is it still No.2?

What was the best thing before sliced bread?

Why is there always a teaspoon in the sink after you've finished doing the washing up?

Why doesn't glue stick to the inside of the tubes?

What is so daft about brushes?

Is there anything that would NOT be 'cheap at half the price'?

Doesn't 'expecting the unexpected' make the unexpected expected?

If love is blind, how can we believe in love at first sight?

If love is blind, why is lingerie so popular?

Why do you have to put your two cents' in, yet it's only a penny for your thoughts? And what happens to the change?

Will the term 'spending a penny' ever be replaced by 'Euro-nating' in the UK?

If the truth is 'out there', what are you doing here?

Why does the Alphabet Song and Twinkle Twinkle Little Star have the same tune? Which came first?

Why did you just try singing the two songs mentioned above?

What if there were no hypothetical questions?

If Men are from Mars, and Women are from Venus, how did we all end up on Earth?

Why do we have jumbo shrimp and freezer burn?

Why is it that no plastic bag will open from the end on your first try?

Clothing Misfits

How can anything other than a glove fit like a glove?

Why is bra singular but panties are plural?

Why is it called lipstick when your lips can still move freely?

If blind people wear dark glasses, shouldn't deaf people wear ear muffs?

If people have vision impairments, why do they wear glasses with dark lenses? Surely this hinders their vision even further.

Shouldn't women wear night gowns to night clubs rather than evening gowns?

Should overweight people refer to their undergarments as 'larges' rather than 'smalls'?

Do boxers wear boxer shorts?

Why do we put suits in a garment bag and garments in a suitcase?

What is so cute about a button?

If you can buy women's tights/stockings in the oddly-named shade 'barely black', why don't they come in equally odd colours such as 'almost almond', 'nearly navy blue', 'roughly red', 'maybe magnolia', 'bordering on brown', 'approaching amber', 'quite quicksilver', 'possibly plum', 'vaguely violet', etc.

Does The Little Mermaid wear an algae-bra?

How do you know if someone is wearing a really good quality camouflage jacket?

Why do people only snag/catch their clothing on door handles when they are in a bad mood?

When A NATO general gives a press conference and takes to the stage in front of the world's media, why does he bother to wear camouflage and, more importantly, why does he bother to wear camouflage which clearly doesn't work?

When on holiday, does a poor dancer, or someone else who can be described as having two left feet, go to a seafront shop and buy a pair of flip flips?

Why is taking the skin off an animal called 'dressing', but taking our clothes off is called 'undressing'?

Why aren't there any bullet-proof pants to go with the vests?

Why do we 'do' our zips up, but we don't 'do' our zips down?

Why are the buttons on men's shirts on the opposite side to those on women's garments?

Where can you buy those little plastic ends to put on your shoe laces and replace the ones that inevitably, and so easily, come off?

What does the 'T' in T-shirt mean?

On Gilligan's Island, how did Ginger have so many different outfits when she was only originally going on a three-hour tour?

Why do overalls have belt loops since they are held up at the top by the straps?

Why are women's and men's show sizes different?

Why are there pictures of the sun wearing sunglasses, when the purpose of sunglasses is to protect your eyes from the sun?

Crime and Pun-ishment

If police arrest a mime artist, do they still give him the right to remain silent, or is he given the right to speak?

If a deaf person is summoned to appear in court, is the proceeding still referred to as a hearing?

If crime doesn't pay, how do you explain lawyers?

How do we know that there's no such thing as a perfect crime?

Why do they bother to sterilise needles for lethal injections?

How important does someone have to be before their death is considered to be an assassination rather than murder?

Do drugs get into schools through supply teachers?

Does Class A in every school have the biggest drugs problem?

Why do police describe a case as open and shut? What other kind of cases are there?

If a midget fortune teller escapes from prison, is he regarded as a small medium at large? And will police hunt high and low for him?

How do police officers handcuff a one-armed man?

If someone with a multiple personality disorder threatened to kill himself, is this considered to be a hostage situation?

Are prisoners allowed to use cell phones?

If a man who was about to be executed in the electric chair has a heart attack on the way there, does anybody try to save him? And if so, would they use a defibrillator?

Do court room cleaners frequently have a brush with the law?

Why do we kill people for killing people in order to suggest that killing people is wrong?

Is the fact that there are so many Australians in the UK conclusive proof that criminals really do return to the scene of the crime?

Do prison buses have emergency exits?

If honesty is the best policy, what is second best? And how do you know if honesty is the best policy, unless you've tried some of the others?

When police cannot identify a body, they often say they are going to have to rely on dental records. But how do they know which dentist to approach?

If crimefighters fight crime and firefighters fight fires, what do freedom fighters fight?

Do you need to use a silencer if you are going to shoot a mime?

Why do banks leave their vault doors open, yet chain their pens to the counters?

Can a homeless man be put under house arrest?

If you steal a clean slate, does it go on your record?

If a criminal turns himself in, can he claim the reward money?

Can a competent criminal be accused of committing a 'decent' assault?

Why did they used to put pictures of criminals up in the Post Office? Do they want members of the public to write to these people? Why don't they put their faces on stamps, to that delivery staff can look for them while they are doing their rounds?

If someone vanished without a trace, how do you know they are missing?

When referring victims of sexual offences to emotional counselling, should they check the signs on the door of the expert first, to ensure that there isn't a typo which makes it read 'the rapist' instead of therapist?

If you walked into your local bank branch and stole a pen, would this still be considered a bank robbery?

If you are in a court of law, and you are asked to tell "the truth, the whole truth and nothing but the truth", what if you say "no"?

If you call the police station to speak to a specific officer, and he or she is not there, is this is what is officially known as a cop out?

Is the term unsolved mystery over-egging things a bit, since if the matter was solved, then it would not be a mystery?

Is a hermaphrodite criminal sent to a men's prison or women's prison upon conviction?

Film Quips and TV Teasers

Posers from 'the pictures', which could almost have filled a book by themselves.

In the movies, why does back-up always arrive the split second after the hero has killed the bad guy?

Do mimes prefer watching silent movies?

If Wile E Coyote can afford to buy all that ACME rubbish, surely he has enough money to buy himself a slap-up meal?

Why is the Lone Ranger called 'lone' when he always had Tonto with him?

Who do people contact if they want to make a complaint about the BBC TV consumer programme 'Watchdog'?

Can you get arrested for running into a fire station and shouting "Movie! Movie!"

How is it that Tarzan is almost always clean-shaven?

How can the hero of a movie survive a brutal beating while displaying little outward signs of pain, but winces noticeably when a woman tries to clean his wounds?

Why is it that, in the movies, when a woman is on the verge of death, the hero simply holds her closely rather than call an ambulance or try to get help?

If Superman can catch bullets in his hands, or let them simply bounce off of his chest, why does he duck when a gun is thrown at him?

In the movies, why does lipstick rarely rub off, and people wake up with perfect hair and make-up?

When being chased over level terrain in the movies, why do most women still manage to fall over?

After making mad passionate love all night long, and exploring every part of each other's bodies, why do movie lovers feel the need to cover themselves with a blanket when they slip out of bed in the morning?

In old war movies, why do German officers speak with a German accent but in perfect English? Shouldn't they be speaking German?

Why do some movie cars burst into flames the moment they barely touch a feather, but a car or helicopter containing a main hero is almost indestructible?

Why is it that main characters can always find convenient parking spaces right outside the places they are visiting, even in the busiest of cities?

Why do people never spot the suspicious car pull out behind them as soon as they pull away from one of those too convenient parking spaces? And isn't it amazing that the pursuers are equally successful in finding a convenient parking space?

In musicals, when someone walks down the street and seemingly spontaneously bursts into song, how is it that everyone around them also knows all the words and the right dance steps?

Why don't the red-suited security guards on board the Starship Enterprise grab a different coloured shirt before beaming down on a mission, considering that the fatality rate for those in red is so very high?

Despite having an obvious numerical advantage and, in theory, being able to easily overwhelm/capture their quarry, why do martial arts villains all wait patiently to launch their attack one at a time?

When involved in a hijacking, an alien invasion, volcanic eruption or other extremely dramatic event, how is it that no one ever seems to go into shock on the silver screen?

When the powers that be on film find a new partner for a cop, how is it that they always seem to manage to find one with a personality which is exactly the total opposite of that cop?

If people in the films can pick locks with credit cards and hairpins in the blink of an eye, why aren't they able to do it when the building is on fire and someone is trapped inside?

Why is it that, even without a British native being present, foreign characters on film still speak to each other in English?

Why do professional, apparently highly-skilled, hitmen, invariably miss with their first shot, yet a woman who has never handled a gun before in her entire life is able to kill the baddie at her first attempt?

How amazing is it that, in a movie, someone switches on a TV at the precise second that a news bulletin starts about an item relevant to the story line? The sense of timing is uncanny...

Why does a single, quick, thrust from a sword instantly kill an extra, but a main character gets the time for a final monologue before the wound proves fatal?

Why is it that people in the soaps/movies never talk about watching soaps/movies?

Why does applause come in rounds?

When shooting at someone who has a bullet-proof vest on or a small round shield or some other form of protection, why does no one ever seem to aim for their unprotected knees or ankles?

When a police officer or movie hero goes to the top of a building because there is someone on the ledge about to throw themselves off, why do they always hesitate when the person says "stop, or I'll jump!" Isn't this what they're intending to do anyway?

If a comedian isn't remotely funny, does he get branded as a 'sit-down' comedian who cheers you down?

If a performer was mediocre, should he or she expect to receive a squatting ovation?

If all the world's a stage, where is the audience sitting?

When you watch a TV programme about ghosts, do you find yourself wondering what is on the other side?

What was Captain Hook's name before he lost his hand?

Why does Bugs Bunny walk around the cartoon world naked but as soon as he goes swimming, he puts on a bathing suit?

Why is it that when Bruce Banner transforms into the Incredible Hulk, his shirts are ripped to shreds but his trousers always seem to stretch?

Can all those intelligent, sharp-eyed newspaper reports at the Daily Planet surely not see through Clark Kent's amazing disguise of a pair of glasses and the hiding of his little curl at the front?

Why does Superman bother to "leap over the tallest building in a single bound", when he can actually fly?

Why couldn't the professor on Gilligan's Island fix a boat, if he could make a radio out of coconuts?

Why are so many American TV police chiefs black?

Why is Mickey Mouse bigger than his dog, Pluto?

Why does Goofy stand erect while Pluto remains on all fours, when they are both dogs?

Why does Superman and so many other superheroes insist on wearing their underwear on the outside?

When a police officer is on his way to a crime, and he spots another crime being committed while on his way, does he stop or does he continue to the original crime?

Why is it that police officers don't wear seatbelts, when we get fined if we don't? Are they not able to be thrown from their cars, too?

In movies and TV shows, what exactly do the 'extras' talk about in the background?

Why is it that you are in a movie but you are on TV?

Why are there no adverts on TV for pencils?

Why, in medicine commercials, do the people use the medicine that does not work first, when they already own the fully-working version?

If The Flintstones is set 'BC', and before American society, as we know it, was founded, how can they have a Flintstones Christmas and Flintstones Thanksgiving?

What would happen if someone put a lightsaber in water?

Why does Donald Duck wear a towel when he comes out of the shower, yet usually doesn't wear any pants?

Why does Mickey Mouse wear pants and no shirt but Donald Duck wears a shirt and no pants?

Why aren't the arm rests between seats in cinemas wide enough to accommodate two elbows?

Why are all the spells in Harry Potter in Latin, when everyone speaks English?

Why doesn't Winnie-the-Pooh ever get stung by the bees he messes with?

If Winnie-the-Pooh was civilised enough to keep his honey in jars, why did he eat if off his hands? Surely he knew how to use a spoon?

If nobody buys a ticket for a movie, does the cinema still screen it?

Do move producers still say "lights, camera, action" when it's a night scene?

When he goes to the bathroom, how does Freddy Kreuger safely wipe his backside?

If the Wicked Witch of the West melts in water, how was she ever able to take a shower or bathe?

If the hit TV show Fantasy Island truly granted wishes to people, why wasn't little Tattoo more than six feet tall?

Why are commercials to subscribe to satellite TV shown on satellite TV and not on non-subscription, regular, TV channels? Don't they want any new customers?

Why are long-running TV series called soap operas, when nobody sings?

Why is it almost always raining and very grey in any funeral scene in a movie or TV show?

How are lead characters always able to get the same table in a café or restaurant in a film?

Why is it that someone who has a nightmare in a movie always wakes up suddenly, sits bolt upright, in a pool of cold sweat, and lets out a short fearful exhalation?

Why do movie characters never take their shoes off when they lie down in bed to think or read a book?

Why is it that someone can always find a spare car key under a sun visor in a movie?

Isn't it funny how movie characters can crack codes so quickly, and are almost instantly able to crack someone else's password, which is usually an important date or pet's name?

Isn't it funny how aliens almost always arrive on earth to attack and invade, they're rarely on a peaceful, diplomatic, mission?

Isn't it funny how one bullet in the right place will instantly detonate a car in a movie, creating a sudden ball of flame?

Why does no one ever seem to lock their cars or the doors of their houses in the movie?

Why does no one in the soaps seem to have normal, nine-to-five, jobs, or play sport on a Saturday afternoon, or listen to the radio, or do normal things?

Why are film characters so wasteful when it comes to food and drink? When was the last time you saw someone finish a meal, or leave an empty glass on the bar, rather than half of the drink that was poured for them a split second beforehand?

Wouldn't it be great if we are down on our luck and our lives had a montage section, a few minutes of toil and sweat after which our strength, talent, fortunes have been transformed for the better?

Why is it that, when there is a group in a movie, they always walk parallel to each other, and there is never anyone behind or in front?

Isn't it convenient that, whenever someone comes up against a door protected by a digital security system in a film, they simply shoot it and it opens?

Why is it that, in real life, applause can break out spontaneously and throughout a crowd, but in a movie it always starts with a slow hand clap from one or two people before then erupting from a whole crowd?

Isn't it great that when someone steals a car in a film, it always has a full tank of fuel?

Isn't it amazing that there can be a confrontation in the toilets of a restaurant or nightclub in the movies, and that, despite the premises being full outside, there is nobody else in the toilet at the time of the confrontation?

More uncanny movie timing! Isn't it amazing that someone can be locked inside a toilet cubicle when two other people come in and start talking about them, usually not in a particularly good way?

Isn't it amazing how movie characters lose their hearing whenever they take a shower?

Isn't it amazing how the whole family gathers for breakfast in the movies? When did that last happen in real life? In saying that, there is usually one member of the family who takes one bite from one slice of toast, despite a veritable feast being laid out on the table, before leaving the house!

When a movie protagonist needs to gain confidence, they seem to look in the mirror? Does it speak back to them, like the magic mirror in Snow White? If so, what does it say in order to instill that further confidence?

Isn't it amazing how the best friend or friends of a main character seem to live very shallow lives themselves; in fact, their lives mostly revolve around the main character, being at their beck and call?

Isn't it amazing how someone who spontaneously leaps from a tall building ends up in a dump truck full of cushioning bags of rubbish, or a truck full of sand which just happens to be passing at the most opportune moment? It's almost as if life was scripted...

Isn't it amazing how so many movie cops have some emotional baggage or a troubled background to contend with? The drink or drugs problem, the dead partner, the unsolved crime, the bitter divorce, the estranged child, the friend-who-betrayed-him who is now back, the woman who broke his heart? Why can't there be a lead character who has a normal, happy, life outside of the job?

How do the superhero teams earn a living and pay their bills? How do they combine all their superhero antics in between apparently having normal jobs? They must have appalling attendance records and very forgiving managers?

How is it that movie characters always seem to live within sight of a city's iconic landmarks, like the Eiffel Tower, Golden Gate Bridge, etc?

Why does a major character yell "no!" when witnesses a tragic moment, as if the word might prevent it from happening?

Why does snowfall in movies always comprise of big, fluffy, flakes?

Are all movie padlocks sold with a gun rather than a key, since they are mostly shot open, and never unlocked in the conventional way?

Why do most movie villains deny their real names when confronted. Often they'll saying something like "once maybe, in another life", or "that person died a long time ago."

Why do movie characters finally get to kiss the girl of their dreams, only to wake up and find a slobbering dog all over them?

Is it true that the main way to solve a problem in Hollywood is to go to a bar and drink yourself into oblivion or, apparently, clarity!

Why do henchmen and extras suffer instant deaths - they may be briefly jabbed by a sword, yet died straight away - yet a key character gets to have a final monologue before passing?

When someone on film receives an email, why do their screens always show a large letter 'e' or an envelope when this is not how email works in the real world?

Why does no one seem to use the mouse or touchpad of their computers in the movies? They just type feverishly on the keyboard.

How is it that, in the movies, everyone seems to have super-fast, state-of-the-art computers and perfect broadband signals?

Isn't it amazingly convenient that when spaceships designed and created by races and species who have never had any contact with each other before are able to dock perfectly?

Why is it that when someone switches on a computer in the movies, it responds almost instantly? Why does no one get a message saying "preparing updates, please don't switch off your computer" or something like that?

Isn't it funny how all movie archaeologists look a bit like Indiana Jones?

Why is it that whenever a henchman or thug is knocked out, the first thing that wakes up is their hand?

Why is there always a gap, passage, tunnel in a sci-fi space ship chase that is almost too tight for the craft to enter?

Why does anyone who is stranded on an island in the movies almost always see at least one aircraft and two boats that they are not able to catch the attention of?

Why do so many villains get their come-uppance by falling from a great height, or, totally coincidentally - apparently - by dying in a way which reflects the way in which they killed someone previously?

Why doesn't the father of any major movie character immediately hide their rare or valuable cars, as it will inevitably be stolen or wrecked or both!

Why is it that, during a movie car chase, cars smash through boxes and bags of rubbish which seem to contain very clean rubbish?

Isn't it amazing how, during a high-speed car chase in a heavily pedestrianised area, people are always able to leap out of the way of speeding vehicles?

Why is it that a couple's kiss is almost always interrupted by a phone call, a knock on the door or someone walking in on them?

When people design buildings, do they purposely install large ventilation tunnels and grilles so that people can escape and crawl through them when necessary?

Why is it, in the movies, that when some tries not to look or act in a suspicious way, they look more suspicious than ever?

Why is it, in the movies, that people don't look where they're going? A soldier in a life-threatening situation retreats backwards without looking where they are going but isn't it amazing how they often bump into someone who turns out to be a friend, not a foe?

Have you ever noticed how people in the movies rarely say goodbye at the end of a phone call? Is it the case that good manners don't exist?

Isn't it funny how Robin Hood and his merry men live in a forest, yet their clothes are, more often than not, very clean and well-pressed and their hair clean and free-flowing?

Why is it when Robin Hood and Maid Marion kiss in the forest, she doesn't recoil because he hasn't cleaned his teeth for who knows how long, and his breath most likely is not particularly pleasant?

Why do TV sports commentators describe a player and say "he can really play football". Well, isn't THAT convenient? If he was an award-winning baker, he probably wouldn't score many goals for his team?

Why is it that, in the movies, someone chases a particularly dangerous individual and ends up in a dark alley or abandoned warehouse, they lose their gun, and have no phone signal at all?

Why do movie characters take pills by clapping them violently into their mouths? Does this make the medicine act quicker?

Why it is TV and movie cops can pace backwards and forwards in front of an investigation board, then destroy it in a fit of rage before spotting something among the mess which, when nice and tidy on the board, had apparently not come to their attention before, and on the back of this they are able to solve the case?

Have you noticed how often a nerdy character explains something complicated to a non-nerd, who replies "in English, please"?

Why do so many alien invasions in movies involve a blue sky beam?

Why do people in the movies slowly submerge themselves in their bathwater completely, before staring dreamily at the ceiling?

If people in the movies had any sense, surely they would have learned to look behind them before closing the mirrored bathroom cabinet door, as otherwise there will almost always be the reflection of someone in the glass as soon as they close the door?

Why do mirrors bring out people's temper, as so many of them get smashed in a fit of rage in the movies?

Isn't it great how movie psychopaths keep scrapbooks, since they will help clear up any ambiguities when it is discovered towards the end of the film?

Have you ever marvelled at how, during a car chase, other cars on the road are all driving much slower and are conveniently staggered to allow the faster cars to weave in and around them safely?

Why is it that an older wiser man who gives advice in the movies generally ends with "you've got a lotta heart, kid"?

Why is it, in the movies, that when trying to defuse a bomb, someone never cuts the first wire they place the cutters around?

Have you ever noticed how, in movies, someone can wiggle the steering wheel of a car left and right without the vehicle moving at all, and still be able to look at the passenger and talk, without hitting anything?

Why does movie rain always fall straight down?

In long-running TV sci-fi series, why does everyone dress the same? What on earth happened to the fashion industry?

Why do the 'bars' on space ships seem so devoid of atmosphere and life, especially if they are the only ones on the ship?

Considering the amazing technology, why is there never a queue outside the holodecks on the Starship Enterprise? You'd have thought it would be the 'go-to' place for off duty crew members.

In shows like Star Trek, all the key crew members are on duty at the same time - the Captain, the number one, the security chief. Who runs the ship during the other times?

Why are galactic bars rough and tumble hovels and dens of iniquity, full of scum and villainous low-lives. Are there no fun pubs or family-friendly restaurants in the future/in space?

During a movie car chase why, at some point, will a car enter a narrow street and inevitably come up against a reversing truck?

Isn't it an amazing coincidence that someone takes a high vantage spot in a movie, and their pursuer always stops directly beneath them, allowing them to drop onto them and gain the upper hand?

Why does anyone in the movies who is immersed in water, or who accidentally falls into water, will always squirt a jet of water from their mouth while recovering, with a look of tired resignation?

Why does anyone on foot who is being chased by a car always try to escape by running up the middle of the road?

Why does someone, in a remote house late at night, hear a suspicious noise and asks "is that you…" knowing full well that, whoever it is they have just named would not be creeping around suspiciously at that time of night.

Have you noticed that, during a movie shoot-out, all bullets make a ricochet sound, even if they miss the target?

Why are all bullets which are surgically removed from someone in films or TV shows have to be dropped into metal kidney dishes?

Why is it that whenever the cloud uncovers a bright moon on the silver screen, an owl hoots?

Have you noticed how, in war movies, if a soldier start writing home about his impending marriage, he will die in battle shortly afterwards?

Have you noticed how someone, usually a spouse, having not believed their other half, turns up late to the courtroom/stage performance etc, sneaks in at the back meets the eyes of their partner and exchanges a look that says they now accept the other's point of view.

Why are all movie security guards completely useless, playing cards, looking at porn magazines, with torches that don't work and keys they keep dropping?

Why, in the movies, must all fuel gauges be tapped to see if they are working properly?

When playing Russian roulette in the movies, why does the one chamber containing a bullet never fire first?

When a team of soldiers run into an armoury to get their weapons in a movie, why is there always a very over-enthusiastic person on hand to distribute the weapons?

Why is it that when someone starts to freak out, someone else slaps them hard to calm them down? Surely in real life, this is likely to make things worse, as not only is the person freaking out freaking out about something, they are now in pain from being hit and are likely to be rather annoyed about that?

Why is it that any solo space traveller who crash-lands onto an unknown world finds himself a short distance from the only other human previously marooned there, but between them will be an enormous carnivore?

In the movies, when a man proclaims his love for a woman, telling her he can't live without her and she's the only thing he needs in life, why is that the woman then always runs in for a kiss?

When playing cards in the movies, how is it that a whole load of professional card sharks get eliminated, leaving the main hero - often a card novice - facing the main villain in a final showdown. What are the chances of the cards falling like that?

In the movies, when an American protagonist gets into a taxi in a foreign city, why does the driver either mention a famous old US actor like John Wayne or starts singing a terrible rendition of New York, New York?

In the movies, even if you're driving on a dirt track, how is it that your tyres still screech when cornering at speed?

When a woman in the movies announces "the baby is coming now!" isn't it amazing that she's right; there's not prolonged period of labour in the films.

Why does a movie police officer commonly declare "I didn't sign up for this" when he actually probably did.

Why is it that, in the movies, explosive decompression on a plane will cause the overheard lockers t open, and they all appear to be full of loose paperwork, although no one could be seen stuffing reams of loose papers into the bins when the plane was boarding?

In the movies, how is it that a computer hack - with no help from their mouse or trackpad - only needs about 30 seconds before being able to triumphantly announce "we're in!"?

Why are so many movie dates arranged with the phrase "I'll pick you up at eight", usually with no address given. Also, isn't this rather late? It means it's likely to be at least nine before they start eating…

Why is it that no one seems to have to wait for a cab in the movies, there is always one on hand to conveniently show up?

How is it that women can walk/run in heels for hours on end in the movies?

Isn't it amazing that movie bartenders seem to remember exactly what drink each customer is having at any given point?

Isn't it clever how, in the movies, a performer can easily pick out a loved one/friend/enemy in a large crowd, despite the stage lights in their faces and all the sound etc.

How is it that all the houses in movies come with amazing L-shaped sheets that are always able to cover up a woman's breasts while she is in bed, while leaving the chest of the man next to her totally exposed?

Have you ever noticed how, in movies set more than a century ago, everyone seems to have such perfect teeth?

Have you noticed how, in the movies, London is almost always foggy?

Why do so many movie bad guys have an English accent?

Isn't it amazing how the FBI arrives in the movies by helicopter, no matter where they have come from?

Why, in the movies, is the immediate reaction of anyone in the path of something life-threatening to stand completely still and stare at it?

Why is it that the biggest and apparently strongest soldier in a team will die first, and the apparently weakest officer will almost always survive?

Why do people in horror movies always take the course of action they have been explicitly advised to avoid?

Isn't it amazing how remote places of the world in movies almost always contain giant versions of animals, and plenty of previously un-discovered creatures?

It always seems remarkably easy to open the door of an aircraft while it's in flight; is this really the case? (If so, I don't think I'm ever going to fly again!)

Why is it that any drug deal in the movies almost always involves multiple fatalities?

Why does reading a book aloud in the movies usually have catastrophic consequences?

Have you ever noticed that you are much more likely to fall from the roof of a moving train in a movie if that train is crossing a very high bridge with a river below?

Isn't it amazing how many horses in the movies appear to be both bullet proof and arrow proof?

Isn't it amazing that two craft meeting in deep space almost always agree what orientation is up and down instinctively?

Why do so many people in the movies who don't know their parentage turn out to be either very rich or aristocracy?

Why is it that all expeditions in movies are led by old and experienced guides with facial scars who usually die horribly before the end?

How is it that spies can hide their 'real occupation' by driving the most expensive cars, eating in the top restaurants, staying in the most luxurious hotel suites and having the most expensive tailored clothing?

Why does a movie villain resist an opportunity to easily kill the hero, justifying this by saying that the hero "might be useful" at some point.

Why do people who retire in the movies almost always buy a boat?

In a movie mountain-climbing expedition, have you noticed how those scared of heights will generally be fine, but the experienced and confident climber will plunge to their death?

Isn't it amazing how women who are reduced to wearing a man's shirt as a dress in a film will always easily find a suitable belt to accessorize?

Why is it that a hero who is being pummeled so often asks, "is that the best you can do?"

Have you noticed how explosive devices in the movies almost always have a handy visual timer and a sneaky redundant circuit to fool anyone who is trying to defuse it?

Have you noticed how the chief henchman will always have some kind of quirk or distinguishing feature, be it a steel bowler hat, a particular scar or tattoo, or some other feature that sets him apart from his cannon-fodder colleagues?

Why is it that grenades are given plenty of time to explode even if the idea is to throw them just before they go off?

When the hero destroys something in a spectacular explosion, why does he never watch his handiwork? He's either walking or driving away, looking in the opposite direction.

Why do men who have been wrongly imprisoned in the movies never seem to have anyone waiting to meet them when they are released?

During a bank robbery in the movies, why to the bank tellers always give away the location of the panic button by glancing at it repeatedly until they catch the eye of a robber, who warns them not to press it?

Have you noticed how many young cops in movies carry semi-automatic pistols while veterans are armed with pump-action shotguns?

Have you noticed how easy it is to knock someone out using blunt force trauma or asphyxiation without causing any permanent damage?

Have you noticed how a girl who is given a firearm in a film either grew up on a farm or learns incredibly quickly when given the briefest of training on how to aim, fire and re-load?

Why is it that, when running away from a falling object such as a tree or stone column in the movies, someone never runs to the side, but always in the same direction as the falling object. If they are not an essential character, they will be crushed. Otherwise they will just be able to cover enough ground to avoid the end of the falling object.

Isn't it amazing how underground trains are just about to leave the station when you arrive on the platform, or the station is totally deserted?

Why do American dads in films seem to think that throwing a baseball at their son is the perfect way to bond and sort out any issues they have been having?

Why does everyone who shops for groceries in an American movie always have a baguette poking out from the top of their bag?

Many explosions in space in the movies feature a huge fireball and a massive bang. How can this be, since there is no atmosphere in space and so no way for sound waves to travel?

Why does someone walk into a bar in the movies ask for a 'beer' without specifying any particular brand?

Have you noticed how, whenever there is an explosion in a film, somebody is running away from it and is just far enough away to be blown off their feet without being seriously hurt.

Why, in movies, does every hostage negotiator ask for one hostage to be released as "a sign of good faith", and his request is almost always granted.

Why is all shopping in the movies carried home in two brown paper bags (one with a baguette sticking out of the top of it), clutched closely to the carrier's chest.

When using a torch in the movies, have you noticed how people hold them like daggers rather than the way people hold them in real life?

Do you think a movie super-villain will ever choose to employ a guard who can actually shoot straight? Isn't it amazing how all dowdy-looking 'plain Jane' women in films simply remove their glasses and let their hair down in order to transform into the most attractive woman in town?

Why is it, in horror films and thrillers, someone is able to make good their escape only to get to a car which refuses to start for at least ten seconds?

Have you noticed how movie cameras following a man climbing down a ladder by tracking from head to toe but will track toe to head with a woman, lingering on her backside?

Why is it that the evil mastermind's right-hand woman will almost always be extremely attracted to the hero of a movie?

Why do people in the movies so rarely need to use the toilet?

Why do all the main villains that James Bond comes up against choose to tell him their entire plan before trying to subject him to an overelaborate means of death which is never going to work in a month of Sundays? If they were truly that evil, why not just shoot Bond between the eyes at the first opportunity?

Why is it that someone can steal a car in the movies by breaking the glass and drive for hours without wincing at being stabbed by a glass splinter?

How is it that so many people know how to hotwire a car and pick a lock in the movies?

Have you noticed how, thanks to what we're taught in the movies, you can apparently survive practically any fall as long as you remember to roll when you land?

Why do movie punches sound like a door being slammed?

Another thing you may have learned from the movies; no matter what your size, shape or level of fitness, it would appear that everyone has the upper-body strength required to not only hang from the ledge of a building for some time, but to pull themselves up over a ledge, too.

Why does a movie moment of grief or anger that begins will a woman pounding on a man's chest with both fists will always end in a passionate kiss?

Have you noticed how large sums of cash are only ever transported in expensive briefcases in the movies?

Why is it that lawn sprinklers are automatically triggered in a film if someone has had his heart broken?

If a movie character has asthma, have you noticed that it is highly likely he will misplace his inhaler at the most inopportune moment?

Have you noticed that most women who have red hair in movies will, at one moment or another, be called Red?

If a small amount of blood is needed for an oath or incantation, why is it obtained by slicing open the palm, which is very painful and which, in the real world, takes forever to heal and hinders a lot of normal use of the hand?

Why do female movie aliens look just human enough to generate some sexual tension between themselves and the human hero?

Why do romantic evenings in the movies require between 150 and 300 candles, depending upon the size of the room?

If someone has a one-night stand in a film before starting a new job, the person they slept with will either be their new boss, a co-worker or the other half of their new boss.

Why is it that someone can be hit in the face with an iron bar, bottle or a fire extinguisher in a film, and yet there is no noticeable damage?

Why is it that, in any struggle with a killer on film, there will be a gun just out of reach?

Have you noticed how, when someone returns to their large house in the movies, every side lamp and small light is switched on in every room?

Why do movie car chases never take place during the rush hour, when the city will be extremely congested with traffic? Yet a cop who is being sent on a mission from phone box to phone box will encounter countless traffic jams, road works, and other obstacles.

Have you noticed how, in a film, a shotgun blast will knock the victim up to 50 feet backwards and yet the shooter remains upright, feet rooted the very spot from which he took the shot.

Are all coffee tables sold in America bullet-proof? It would appear so, since an overturned coffee table in a film seems able to stop a hail of gunfire.

Isn't it amazing that a car can mount a pavement during a high-speed chase in a film, but do no more harm than knock over some fruit stands and disrupt a few alfresco diners?

How is it that, in the movies, a speeding car is ridiculously easy to hold onto, especially if you've just jumped on top of one from another speeding vehicle?

Isn't it amazing how, in movies, the only person with vital information that is way too sensitive to share by email or phone, will be on their way to relay that information in person when their car is broadsided by a very heavy lorry?

Have you noticed how complex problems are never solved in films without someone telling a seemingly completely unrelated story until the disinterested hero then uttering, "wait, say that again"?

Should you be wary of surrogate mothers, since movies suggest that all such people are evil? In any movie chase involving dozens of police cars (just how many cars does each police department have? It seems like they must have a constant production line of them!), why is it that at least three of them will flip over and roll wildly for no apparent reason?

Have you noticed how high school parties in movies never have fewer than 200 guests?

Why is it that, when someone is handcuffed to a chair, it's often a wooden, poorly-constructed, chair which is going to prove quite easy to escape from? Why does the captor not realise this?

Isn't it fortunate that, in the movies, there is almost always someone around who still knows Morse Code?

Isn't it convenient (pun intended) that all public bathrooms in movies have windows just big enough to climb out of, while private bathrooms are hermetically sealed so that if water is left running, it will pool up until someone opens the door, causing a torrent to flood out.

In any movie wedding, why is there a much higher than average chance of someone not showing up, or someone publicly declaring their love for the bride or groom, or of someone falling into the cake?

How is it that you are able to get into pretty much any building in a movie if you are dressed as a flower delivery person?

Have you noticed how often a nerdy character explains something complicated to a non-nerd, who replies "in English, please"?

Have you noticed how people in the movies wake up in hospital and are immediately alert enough to be able to pull out their IV drips?

Why do so many alien invasions in movies involve a blue sky beam?

Are you aware of the rule of proportionality in the movies: the more diabolical the villain, the more dramatic his death will be?

Isn't it amazing how, in the movies, defibrillators can bring people back to life, even when they're not being used properly?

Is it true that the meanest movie bad-asses all have long coats?

During a legal proceeding in a film, why is a lawyer either woefully corrupt, or involved in his first court-room appearance?

How is it that female teachers in films are either elderly or inappropriately sexy, while male teachers come in all varieties?

Have you noticed how most movie bank robberies start with a gun being shot at the ceiling? It's also highly likely that at least one member of the criminal gang is dangerously unstable.

Have you noticed how, in the movies, despite living in a post-apocalyptic wasteland for who knows how long, women have groomed eyebrows, perfect teeth and hairless legs?

Why do female warriors rarely go into battle in the films with their hair pulled back? Doesn't it get in their way?

Why is it that if a woman vomits in a film, it's almost always an indication of pregnancy?

Have you noticed how often people in films are seen apparently drinking from cups which are quite clearly empty?

Food For Thought

Where is the flap in a flapjack?

Why is it called a round of toast, when it's most frequently served as squares or triangles? And considering that most bread is square, why is sandwich meat most commonly round?

Why are chillies called chillies when they're actually hot?

If man was not meant to indulge in midnight feasts, why do refrigerators have lights inside them?

If oranges are called oranges because they are orange, why aren't limes called greens, lemons called yellows and tomatoes called reds? And come to that, why are carrots often far more orange than oranges?

Why don't they make bigger tins for sardines, or just put fewer fish into each tin?

Why do people call rare steak 'blue' when it is actually really rather red?

Is a square meal a TV dinner? And why do people eat square meals from round plates?

What's the point of a dry drink?

Why do containers of sour cream have an expiry date printed on them?

Is a balanced diet having a chocolate cake in each hand?

What did cured ham have before it was cured? And if it is cured, can you still catch food poisoning from it?

If man was not meant to eat animals, why are they all made out of meat?

If you buy a bag of new potatoes from the supermarket and they exceed their 'use by' date, what do you now call them?

Why is vanilla ice cream white or yellow, when vanilla extract is brown?

How quick to you need to cook for something to be considered fast food?

During your first few weeks at a slimming club, are you just finding your feet?

Why are round pizzas always delivered in square boxes?

If you eat a diet of food which is full of preservatives, will you live longer?

Why do sandwiches and toast cut into triangles taste better than square pieces?

If you ate pasta and antipasti, would they cancel each other out, meaning that you don't gain weight but that you're also very hungry?

Does condensed milk come from smaller cows?

Why are 'plain crisps' referred to commonly as 'ready salted'? With the exception of those packets which contain the little blue bags of salt, aren't most packets of crisps ready-flavoured? Why do they feel the need to emphasise this on the pre-salted ones?

Why does lemon juice and lemonade often contain artificial ingredients while washing-up liquid apparently contains "real lemons"?

If white wine goes with fish, do grapes go best with sushi?

If vegetarians only eat vegetables, what do humanitarians feed on? Could it be that humanitarian is actually another word for cannibal?

If you soak a raisin in water, does it turn back into a grape?

Why does grapefruit look nothing like a grape?

What do illiterate people make of alphabet soup?

Are kidneys shaped like beans or beans shaped like kidneys?

If you eat a chocolate bar and nobody sees you, does it have any calories?

Why don't we simply cut out the middle man and flush sweetcorn kernels straight down the toilet?

What on earth prompted someone to prise open an oyster, examine the contents and think "doesn't this look delicious?"

Was it the same man who looked at a cow and thought "I'll squeeze those dangly things and drink whatever comes out?"

Presumably, it was also the same man who saw a chicken dispense an egg from its arse and think "it will be good to eat that!"

Why do they put holes in crackers?

What do chickens think we taste like?

Is a drunken/intoxicated ghost a methylated spirit?

If olive oil comes from olives, vegetable oil from vegetables, peanut oil from peanuts and sunflower oil from sunflowers, how do you explain baby oil?

Is it true that someone could not afford to buy a pair of venison because it was two deer?

Is Baked Alaska a sign of global warming?

If we were all meant to be vegetarians, why aren't plants made out of meat?

If vegetarians are opposed to meat products, why do the makers of some foods like Quorn create chicken flavour fillets and sausages? Also, to ensure the flavour is accurate, does it mean that someone has had to taste chicken to make a comparison, and therefore an animal has died in order for the accuracy of the flavour to be ascertained?

Do cannibals avoid eating clowns because they think they taste funny?

Do people not eat parrots because they think the meal will repeat on them?

Why don't greengrocers come in other colours?

Does a cannibal become hungry again just an hour after eating a Chinese person?

If a Cockney wants to buy some apples and pears from a greengrocer, does he ask for some stairs?

Why are the drinks called milkshakes, when they have already been shaken? Shouldn't they be called 'milkshook', or 'milkshaken'?

What does the hotcake seller say when his hotcakes are selling particularly quickly? And just how fast do hot cakes sell?

If Pringles are so good that "once you pop, you can't stop", why do the tubes they come in have re-sealable lids?

Why do black olives come in cans and green olives come in jars?

Why do hotdog sausages commonly come in packs of eight but hotdog buns are commonly sold in packs of ten?

Why do we have brown sauce but tomato ketchup?

Do tee-totallers suffer from hangunders?

If Alcoholics Anonymous really IS anonymous, why do people start the meetings by announcing "hello, my name is…"?

Why are the smaller versions of popular chocolate bars called 'fun' size? Surely, it's much more fun (and satisfying) to eat bigger bars?

If a normal size bar of chocolate is supposed to satisfy you, why do they make king size bars?

Why doesn't 'whoop ass' come in bottles?

If croutons are stale bread, why do they come in airtight packaging?

What happened to the six drinks before they settled on 7Up?

Do male cannibals eat their girlfriends and then dump them?

If terrorists starting using alphabet soup - either containing an explosive or a poison - could this action spell disaster for their enemies?

If a parsley farmer is successfully sued, can the authorities garnish his wages?

Where does all the carrots in vomit come from?

What is the difference between a chip and a French fry?

How do seedless grapes keep going?

If butter is yellow, is a hiccup burple?

If a bottle of poison has an expiry/use-by date, and exceeds it, does it become more poisonous, or does it become safer?

Can vegetarians eat animal crackers?

There are 24 hours in a day and 24 cans of beer in a case. Coincidence?

How does a Thermos know when to keep a hot drink hot and a cold drink cold?

Why do toasters have a setting that burns bread to a horrible blackened crisp that no one in their right mind would want to eat?

Why doesn't a chicken egg taste like chicken, or why doesn't chicken meat taste like eggs?

How did the pineapple get its name, when it has neither pine nor apple in it?

How do you go about cooking the shrimp that live around volcanic fumaroles on the ocean floor, where the temperature is about 500 degrees C? Surely, at this temperature, the shrimp are already cooked? Is this Mother Nature's version of a ready-meal?

If you have a single crumb in front of you in the table and you split it with a knife, do you now have two crumbs or two halves of one crumb?

What's the point of alcohol-free lager and decaffeinated coffee? What is next, pork-free pigs?

How is it that things have got so bad that a pizza can arrive at your house when you've called for one quicker than an ambulance does?

If a supermarket claims to be lowering the prices of some food items every day, surely one of these days some of those items will be free?

Why does Germany make such a big deal out of the quality of its sausages, when it's well-known that German sausages are wurst?

Can it be considered as progress if a cannibal learns to eat with a fork?

Is there a Dr Salt?

Why do people who only eat natural foods drink decaffeinated coffee?

What happens if you put "this side up" face down while popping microwave popcorn?

Why is it that Chinese restaurants serve items called egg rolls which actually have no egg content at all?

Why do people on the North American continent describe their breakfast liquid as 2% Milk when the percentage actually refers to the fat content, not the milk?

Why do donuts have holes?

When someone starts eating Swiss cheese, where do all the holes go?

How is it that there is a breakfast cereal called Grape Nuts which contains neither grapes nor nuts?

Is there a time limit on fortune cookie predictions?

Why do fast-food outlets call their roadside restaurants 'drive thru' when you actually have to stop at them?

Most mothers feed their babies using little plastic spoons and forks. What do Chinese mothers use, toothpicks?

If you butter a piece of toast and drop it, it lands butter-side down. If you drop a cat, it always lands on its feet. What would happen if you buttered the back of a cat and dropped that?

If you put orange juice in the freezer, it becomes frozen. Why then, when you squeeze orange juice, do you not describe as the fruit as squozen?

Why do they print 'serving suggestion' next to the picture of a product on its label? Surely it should be quite obvious?

Do fish ever get cramps after eating?

What happens when you swallow your pride?

If you mix Phillips' Milk Of Magnesia with vodka and orange juice, do you get a Phillip's screwdriver?

If milk goes bad if it's not refrigerated, why don't they refrigerate cows?

Why does the Easter bunny carry eggs, when rabbits don't lay eggs?

Why is there that little space inside strawberries, as if it was meant for a pit, when all the seeds are on the outside?

Can a cannibal be arrested for being under the influence of alcohol if he has just eaten someone who was drunk?

If a cannibal was on death row, could he ask for his last meal to be the last guy who was electrocuted?

Why are plastic bears the only animal you can get honey from? Why can't you get honey from a plastic bee?

If prunes are dehydrated plums, where does prune juice come from?

If the serving size on a can of soda is 'one can', then why is the serving size on a little can 'one can', too? Wouldn't the little cans be "half a can" or the bigger can be two or three cans?

Why do ketchup bottles always instruct you to 'shake well' but there are no such instructions on sachets of exactly the same sauce?

What is a chickpea if it is neither a chick nor a pea?

Why do some peanut butter jars contain the warning, "may contain traces of peanuts"? Surely that goes without saying?

Isn't it strange that you bake cookies but cook bacon?

What was the thinking behind naming pepperoni, when there isn't any pepper in it?

Why aren't French fries considered to be vegetables when all they are is deep-fried potatoes?

Why is most lunchmeat bigger than the bread?

Why do we have to wait until the water starts boiling before we put pasta into it?

People - usually parents - warn you that if you eat dessert before dinner, it will ruin your appetite. If that's true, why doesn't eating dinner ruin your appetite for dessert?

When you go to a burger restaurant, you get charged extra if you add a slice of cheese or bacon to your burger, so why is it that you don't get a discount if you ask for something to be taken off of your burger?

Why do people say "you can't have your cake and eat it, too?" Why would anyone want to get cake if they can't eat it?

Why isn't chocolate considered to be a vegetable, since chocolate comes from cocoa beans and all beans are vegetables?

Why is it that if something says "do not eat" on the packaging, it becomes extra tempting to eat?

Why does the last piece of ice always stick to the bottom of the glass?

Why is there a full English breakfast, but never a full English dinner or tea?

Why isn't evaporated milk a gas?

Once man figured out how to put food into a can, how long was it before they invented the can opener to get it back out again?

Geographical Queries

Where is Old Zealand?

Do people in Australia refer to the rest of the world as 'up over'?

Where are all the second world countries?

How much longer can the Americans keep referring to one of their cities as *New* York?

Are people who are born in Paris known as Parisites?

If people from Poland are called 'Poles', why aren't people from Holland known as 'Holes'?

Do upmarket seaside towns sell rods of marble rather than sticks of rock?

In countries which apparently embrace the philosophy of free speech, why are there phone bills?

What do they call a French Kiss in France?

Do Parisian's ask for 'French Toast' or is it just toast to them, and they can ask for 'English Toast' as an alternative?

Do people in India and China ever pop out for an English?

Is a paddy field where Irishmen grow?

If someone owns a piece of land, do they own it all the way down to the core of the Earth?

Why are outlets electrical but inlets geographical?

If someone started digging a hole, went through the centre of the earth and kept going until they came out on the other side, would they come out feet-first?

If all roads lead to Rome, how do Romans get anywhere else?

Why does the US have a government department called Department of Interior when it is in charge of everything outdoors?

If you lived in Siberia and you wronged the Russian government, where would they send you?

If you got drunk in the UK and then went to the USA, and were still inebriated when you arrived, could they arrest you for underage drinking, even though you didn't consume the alcohol in the US?

If it's 11.30pm on 31 December in Texas but 00.30hrs 1 January in New York, and your New York licence expires at the start of January, has your licence expired or, if you're in Texas, do you still have 30 minutes' use of it?

If we say that something that we don't understand "sounds like Greek to me", what do the Greeks say?

When a French person swears, does he say "pardon my English"?

Why is the country called the People's Republic of China when China is not a republic?

(Un)Healthy Bodies and Minds

Can acupuncture cure pins and needles?

Isn't it a little unnerving that doctors call the place in which they work a 'practice'?

Is half of a large intestine a semi-colon?

If something is considered to not be contagious, how did you catch it in the first place?

If you get called a hypochondriac, does it hurt?

If laughter is the best medicine, how do you explain the phrase "I nearly died laughing?"

Are girls allowed into Guys Hospital?

Is it true that diarrhoea is genetic because it's in your genes?

If diarrhoea only runs down one leg, is it called monorrhoea?

If four out of five people suffer from diarrhoea, does that mean that one in five people actually enjoy it?

If you called the incontinence helpline, what would you do if they asked you to hold? If the line was busy, is this what prompted the use of the word 'engaged' on the doors of occupied public conveniences?

When a woman has twins, are there two umbilical cords?

If the way to a man's heart is through his stomach, wouldn't that cause indigestion? Is this why so many marriages leave a nasty taste in the mouth?

Why doesn't the gene pool have a lifeguard?

Could you be a cardiologist if your heart wasn't in it?

If a doctor has a heart attack during surgery, to the other doctors and nurses in the room work on the doctor or do they continue with the patient?

Can an insomniac be a good anesthetist?

Why does the sun lighten our hair but darken our skin?

Are there any germs which cause good breath?

Why is it called the funny bone, because if you hit it in the right way it makes you want to cry?

Why isn't there a common name for the tops of your feet?

How old are you before it can be said that you died of old age?

What happens if you receive a kidney transplant from someone who was incontinent?

Why do doctors leave the room or pull the curtain when you get undressed, and then return to the room/open the curtain when you are naked and poke, prod and probe you in all sorts of private places?

Why do some stores force sick people to walk all the way to the back of the premises to get their prescriptions while healthy people can buy chocolate, cakes and even cigarettes from the front?

Why does your nose run and your feet smell?

Where does the toe tag go on a dead person who doesn't have any toes?

If you had all the limbs on your left side amputated, would you be alright?

If you're born again, do you have two belly buttons?

Did Roman medics refer to IV lines as 4's?

Why aren't moustaches called mouthbrows?

Does the National Eczema Society raise funds through the use of scratch cards?

Can bald people get hairline fractures?

How is it that you can't get to choose your face, but you can pick your nose?

When people lose weight, where does it go?

Why do people order double cheeseburgers, large fries and then a Diet coke?

If you had X-ray vision and closed your eyes tightly, would you still be able to see?

If you had X-ray vision which meant that you could see through anything, wouldn't you see through absolutely everything, and therefore actually see nothing?

What happened to Preparations A to G?

Why do we call a part of our body the 'bottom' when it's actually a lot closer to the middle?

If a case of 'the clap' spreads more widely, at what point could it be considered a case of the applause?

If an astronaut caught a cold while in orbit, would he still say he was feeling under the weather? Does saying that you feel 'over the weather' mean that you actually feel fine?

Is sweat nature's way of telling you that your body is screaming "no more, no more!"?

Why do doctors instruct you to breathe in and breathe out, since if you were not already doing this, you would probably dead.

Since the doctor invariably says "take two aspirins", why don't they simply make aspirins bigger so that you only need to take one?

Since only women menstruate, wouldn't it be more accurate to describe it as womenstruate?

Why are there never any positive side effects to medication or drugs? Wouldn't the world be a better place if the label on a prescription bottle read, "may cause extreme sex appeal", or "may cause extreme intelligence"?

If you sleep like a baby, does this mean that you wake up screaming every 10 minutes and often wet the bed?

If a child refuses to sleep during nap time, can you charge them with resisting a rest?

Why is it that fingers have tips, toes don't, yet we talk about tip-toeing, not tip-fingering?

Do you yawn in your sleep?

Do you wake up or open your eyes first?

If a person who suffered from amnesia was cured, would they remember that they forgot?

When we say that our mind wanders, where do we think it actually goes?

If you had no imagination, would you be able to pretend that you did?

Could you be a closet claustrophobic?

What happens to you if you get scared half-to-death, twice?

What happens when curly-haired people watch something that would usually make someone's hair curl?

If you are cross-eyed and have dyslexia, can you read all right?

Why do older women blue or pink-rinse their hair? Is it to comfort the older men who lose theirs, so that the ladies can say "just be grateful that you lose it; look what colour it goes if you keep it!"

If, as the advertising would have us believe, the third blade of a best-selling razor shaves you 'even closer' than the first two, what's the point of having the first two there anyway?

Does anybody really have a toffee nose?

Isn't everybody on their last legs?

Why do they call it an asteroid when it's outside the hemisphere and a hemorrhoid when it's inside your ass?

Is the healthier equivalent of a couch potato a comfy-chair chip?

If someone got addicted to counselling, how would you treat them?

Can someone who unsuccessfully tries to kill themselves by taking an insufficient quantity of pills be described as suffering from an underdose?

Can someone who is over-tired use, as an excuse for their lethargy, the fact that they have taken an underdose of stimulants?

What happens if you let a nine-year-old use a beauty product which claims to make you look ten years younger?

Why is navel fluff always blue?

Is 'navel manoeuvres' a posh term for belly-dancing?

Why don't the hairs on your arms get split ends or dandruff?

If you swallow a burp, does it turn into a fart?

If you burp and fart at the same time, does it create a vacuum in your stomach?

If soap is used to make you clean, and is meant to be effective, why does it leave a scum behind?

Sooner or later, doesn't everyone stop smoking?

Can you make a candle out of your earwax?

Why is the 'knee-jerk' response to a paper cut, "Oh, those are the worst kind" when, in fact, getting hacked to pieces by a machete is probably a tad more unpleasant?

Why does hair grow out of men's ears? Is it because it no longer has the strength to make it all the way up to the top of their heads?

Do sore thumbs really stick out?

Why are toe nail clippers bigger than finger nail clippers, yet toe nails tend to be generally smaller than finger nails?

Why does the labelling on sleep-aids such as Nytol contain a warning that the product "may cause drowsiness"? Isn't that the point?

Are eyebrows regarded as facial hair?

If everyone lost five pounds in weight, would it through the earth off of its gravitational axis?

How do painkillers know where the pain is?

What does the back of a tongue look like?

Why do men have nipples?

Why can't you keep your eyes open when you sneeze?

Do narcoleptics ever get over-tired?

If fit people consider their bodies to be 'temples', do fat people think of their bodies as bouncy castles?

Do overweight drinkers consider their ample midriff to be a beer festival rather than a six-pack?

When you snap your fingers, does the sound occur when your middle finger releases from your thumb or when your middle finger hits the palm of your hand?

If your therapist asks you to let your mind go blank, how you would know you had succeeded?

Why do people say they are going to take a dump or a leak; wouldn't they prefer to leave it?

Why are there branded 'disposable douchebags'? Why on earth would you want to keep a douchebag after using it?

Is the height of irony getting a paper cut from a Get Well card?

Can water freeze in your belly during zero-degree weather

Considering there is so much water in the human body, why don't we freeze in zero-degree weather?

If a baby's leg pops out at 23.59hrs and its head comes out at 00.01, what day was he born on?

If someone has their nose pierced, catch a bad cold, and take their nose ring out, does their nasal discharge also come out of the piercing hole when they sneeze?

Why is it that when you're sleeping, it's called drool but when you're awake, it's called spit?

Why doesn't the hair on your arms grow as fast as the hair on your head?

If you only have one eye, are winking or blinking?

If a General is a higher ranking officer than a Major, why is a major illness worse than a general illness?

If your eyes are crossed, do your tears fall straight?

Why do people squint their eyes when they are having trouble seeing? Wouldn't squinting just create even less space to see out of, and make someone's vision even worse?

Can a metal plate which has been inserted into someone's head go rusty? (If so, it could probably explain quite a lot…)

Why to the labels on children's Tylenol warn not to use before work with heavy machinery? How many five-year-olds with headaches do you know who drive fork-lift trucks?

If you only had one hand, would second-hand smoking affect you? Would you go to a second-hand shop?

If an elderly person takes a bath, how do they know if their bodies have been soaking in the tub for too long?

Have you ever wondered what the other side of your belly button looks like?

Home (dis)Comforts

Why do we wash bath towels? Surely we are clean when we use them?

Is a gold-plated knife and fork still considered as silverware?

What to people in China call their good plates?

Do you need to think of a new name if someone dies in your living room?

Would water beds be bouncier if they were filled with spring water?

Why is it that, no matter what vibrant or deep colour the bubble bath solution is, the bubbles themselves are always white? The same applies with shampoo lather!

What would a chair look like if your knees bent the other way?

Why do we leave cars worth many thousands of pounds on our driveways, but fill our garages with useless junk?

Why do you so rarely find artist materials in a drawing room?

If you have a steam room at home and a walk-in fridge, what do you consider to be 'room temperature'?

Why do wire coat hangers seem to multiply in the wardrobe?

Why is it that you spend hours tossing and turning in your bed at night, trying to get to sleep, but as soon as you get to half an hour before it's time to get up, you start sleeping like a log? And, come to that, has anyone ever been around long enough to see a log wake up?

Why do you keep trying to vacuum up a piece of string but when that doesn't work, you pick it up by hand, roll it into a ball and toss it back onto the floor in order to give the vacuum cleaner another chance?

Does a house burn up or burn down?

Don't you have to re-start before refinishing a table?

Why do we have 'hot water heaters' when, by definition, hot water is already hot so doesn't need to be heated any further?

If you sit in front of a bird cage reading a newspaper, does your pet bird wonder why you're just sitting there, staring at his carpet?

If Luke took a bath, would the water be lukewarm?

How do you throw away a garbage can?

Why do we scrub down but wash up?

If you take a shower, where do you take it?

In winter, why do people try to keep their homes as warm as they were in the summer, when they complained about the heat?

Why is it that when you attempt to stop something from falling off the table, you usually manage to knock something else over?

If you play a blank CD/tape/MP3 file at full volume, and you have a mime living next door, would he complain?

Why aren't curtains double-sided, so that it looks nice on the inside and the outside of your home?

Why is almost every brand of toilet bowl cleaner blue?

Why are floor coverings called carpets, when they have nothing to do with cars or pets?

If Round-Up kills grass/weeds, would Square-Down make it grow?

How does Santa get into a house that doesn't have a chimney?

Why do mattresses have designs on them when they're always covered with sheets and very few people get to see them?

If a fold-up table can be propped up, can it also be propped down?

Miscellaneous Mysteries

A collection of assorted imponderables which did not naturally fit into any of the other categories in this compilation.

How can there be *self*-help groups?

Why are toy hippos blue, purple or pink, whereas real hippos are brown?

How do you raise something to the ground?

Where, in the nursery rhyme, does it ever suggest that Humpty Dumpty was a giant egg?

How can something be new AND improved? If it's new, what can it be an improvement on?

If I save time, when do I get it back?

Why aren't marbles made of marble?

Why is it necessary to screw down the lid of a coffin?

If two negatives make a positive, why don't two wrongs make a right?

How do you know which price comparison website will really get you the best deal? Is there a compare the comparison websites website? (It could be called 'gocomparetheconfusedmoneysupermeerkat.com).

Can you dream of having a dream?

How can someone draw a blank?

If it's not your round, does it matter whether the glass is half full or half empty?

If the person who designed the drawing board didn't get it right the first time, what did he go back to?

When the clocks go forward, why does it happen at 1am or 2am on a Sunday morning? Surely the most popular time to put the clocks forward one hour is 4pm on a Friday?

When telling the time, why are some people compelled to say things like "2am in the morning". It wouldn't be the afternoon if it is 2AM, would it?"

If time is such a great healer, how is it that it always kills you in the end?

Isn't it somewhat restrictive to consider the sky to be the limit?

If you keep an open mind, how do you stop everything from falling out?

Which end of the morning is the top?

What do fairies do with all the children's teeth they pay for?

If you dive into a pool of dry ice, can you swim without getting wet?

If vampires don't have reflections in mirrors, how is it that Dracula's hair is always impeccably neat and tidy?

If a US president was involved in a scandal involving someone's private rear lawn, would the matter be referred to as Garden Gate?

If Barbie (the doll) is so popular, why do you have to buy her friends?

Why is it that when I wind up my watch, I am starting it, when I wind up doing something, I am doing it in the present tense, and it is ongoing, but when I "wind up" whatever else I am doing, I am bringing it to an end?

How would people react if someone ran into the Headquarters of the Conservative Party and said, "help, please come quickly, my wife is in Labour?"

Is a bi-monthly magazine a regular publication for people who enjoy sexual relations with both genders?

Why can't women put on mascara with their mouths closed?

Who is 'Larry' and why is he apparently always so much happier than the rest of us?

Who is Will and what did he do to annoy everyone so badly that he became public enemy number one, and is always the first in the firing line?

When people say "I don't know him from Adam", who is Adam and why can't people differentiate between him and anyone else? Is he some kind of human chameleon?

Why do we sing 'rock-a-bye' baby as a comforting lullaby when you consider its violent and tragic ending?

Why don't you get female transvestites?

If you bought a 'bag for life' from a supermarket, would you be able to use it to suffocate yourself?

Does the fact that there is a right angle mean that there are 359 wrong ones?

Where does your lap go when you stand up?

If something was second to none, would you really rather have none?

If something is truly worth doing, wouldn't it have been done already?

What's the point of apathy?

If you can 'agree to disagree', can you 'disagree to agree'?

Can you plan to do something spontaneously?

If tin whistles are made of tin, what are foghorns made of?

When a piece of cheese has its photograph taken, what does it say? Does it shout out "meeeeeee"?

Does history have a future?

Do political parties get gatecrashers?

Is beauty in the eye of the beerholder?

If the cost of living is getting so high, how is it that it still seems so popular?

Who owns the copyright on the copyright symbol?

If today is the first day of the rest of your life, what in the world was yesterday?

Is it true that 93.8% of all statistics are meaningless?

Why doesn't Murphy's Law read: "If something can go wrong, it will go wraongue"?

If it is true, why is change still inevitable?

If the average wasn't mean, would you get more?

If UFOs were proven to exist, would they be re-named IFOs?

Why doesn't a monkey wrench fit monkey nuts?

If the enemy is in range, doesn't that mean that you are, too?

Is an organisation a home for wayward accordions?

Why isn't there a national week week?

If someone said they would kill for a Nobel Peace Prize, do you think they should be award one?

When you open a bag of cotton balls, is the top one meant to be regarded as packaging and thrown away?

If ghosts can walk through walls so easily, why don't they fall through floors?

Surely the correct phrase to describe a conflict is an UNcivil war? Or is a civil war one in which participants are very polite. "I say, old chap, would you mind very much keeping absolutely still while I shoot you to death, there's a good fellow. Thank you so much."

Do burns victims get a discount at the crematorium?

When you go to Disneyland and have your photo taken with one of the characters, is the person inside the Mickey Mouse costume also smiling for the camera?

Why do people say "good grief"? What's so good about it?

Why are circles so vicious when they have no pointy bits or jagged edges?

Do you only get a reprimand after you have been primanded in the first place? And what, exactly, is a 'primand'?

How do you know if you have had a blessing in disguise, unless the disguise in question is a particularly poor one?

Where do all the letters go that get lost in the post?

Is it true that the most severe penalty for bigamy is having *two* mothers-in-law?

If you try to choke a Smurf, what colour does it become?

How many people thought of the Post-It note before it was actually invented, but they didn't have anything to jot their ideas down on?

If you have a bunch of odds and ends, and get rid of all but one of them, what do you call it?

If you spend all day doing nothing, how do you know when you're done?

Shouldn't the correct advice be *some* things in moderation?

Is the best way to save face to keep the lower part of it shut?

How do you know when it's time to re-tune your bagpipes?

If electricity comes from electrons, does morality come from morons?

Why doesn't anybody make the sticky stuff on the back of envelopes taste like chocolate?

Have you noticed that if you re-arrange the letters of the words Mother-in-Law, you get Woman Hitler?

Why were all the blackboards in my old school called blackboards when the vast majority of them were green?

How can there be a limited lifetime warranty?

If Milli Vanilli fell in a forest, would somebody else make a sound?

If practice makes perfect, but nobody's perfect, is there much point in anybody practicing?

Is there an exception to the rule that there's an exception to every rule?

Most packing says "open here", so what would you do if you found a package that said "open somewhere else"?

If you can read the marking, isn't that end already up?

Is a sleeping bag actually a nap sack?

If Jimmy cracks corn and no one cares, why does he keep doing it?

Aren't all generalisations false?

If someone invented instant water, what would they mix it with?

What does it mean if you break a mirror with a rabbit's foot as you walk under a ladder just as a black cat crosses your path?

Are there any female leprechauns?

Why can you never find anywhere to hang a skyhook?

In America, when a man is elected President, his wife is known as the First Lady. When America elects its first female President, what will her husband be known as?

Is the US Vice-President's wife known as the Second Lady?

Does the reverse side also have a reverse side?

If an anarchist group attained political power, would they, by principle, have to dissolve their own government?

Why does the packaging on some sets of Christmas lights say "for indoor or outdoor use only"; as opposed to what, exactly?

Does killing time damage eternity?

Why don't composers and other people just write down the letter of each musical note rather than all those funny little circles?

If man puts a steak on a black eye, what does a cow use?

If you invented an acid that could eat through anything, what would you keep it in?

The Italians have had some of the greatest painters in history, so why did it take a Frenchman to invent their national flag?

Because so many products in stores have prices ending in 99p, whey don't we have a 99p coin?

Were the parents of the seven dwarves normal-sized people? And did they get to seven and then decide to stop trying for a girl?

Why is it that one match can start a forest fire but it takes at least one whole box of matches to light a barbecue?

What happens if someone loses the lost and found box?

Why does the Commission for Racial Equality not have more white people working for it?

Why is it that every time I feel like opening a can of worms, the supermarket is right out of stock?

If the pen is truly mightier than the sword, would I be considered a more honorable man if I allowed an opponent who has challenged me to a duel to wield the pen while I resign myself to having nothing but a sword to defend myself with?

What would happen if an irresistible force met an immovable object?

What would you use to dilute water?

How can military troops be deployed, or redeployed, if they've never been ployed to begin with?

If "I think, and therefore I am", am I just a thought?

Is it a coincidence that the word 'politics' is made up of the word 'poli', which means 'many' in Latin, and 'tics' as in blood-sucking parasites?

When you erase a word with a pencil, where does it go?

Do astronauts change their watches when the move over different time zones while in space?

What happens if a queen gives birth to Siamese twins? Who gets to be succeed her as king?

Do all-boy schools have girls' bathrooms, and vice versa?

Do glow-in-the-dark objects stop glowing when somebody turns the lights on, or do they still glow but we don't notice because it's now so bright?

If you have a gun, and you says "can I ask you a question" and the person you are pointing the gun at says "fire away", should you then shoot that person?

Why are red buttons always the most important?

Can a school teacher give homework to a homeless pupil?

Why aren't safety pins as safe as they claim to be?

Why are people allowed to put naked statues outside, but can't run around naked?

Why is it that you have to turn some products upside down in order to read the directions, and the directions say "do not turn upside down?"

In the song 'She'll Be Coming Round The Mountain', who is she, why is she coming, where is she coming from and what does she want?

Why is there a top line on lined paper if we never use it?

Can you put a gay man into a straight jacket?

Can you 'zone out' and be 'in the zone' at the same time?

If society is so modern and progressive, why is it that, in the 1500s, nude paintings were considered art, whereas today it would be regarded as pornography?

Natural Wonders

Why is wind?

How does a river run?

How deep would the ocean be if there were not any sponges in it?

If someone falls unconscious in the Sahara Desert during a heatwave, do you still say that he is "out cold" or is he "out warm"?

Why does natural mineral water which has, apparently, "trickled through the mountains for centuries", have an expiry date?

What is the speed of dark?

If we have a speed of light and, possibly, a speed of dark, is there also a speed of smell?

Why don't we have cultured and sophisticated oil, rather than just crude oil?

Why is it that rain drops but snow falls?

If there is no gravity on the moon, why don't moon rocks fly around all the time?

Are crop circles the calling card of a cereal killer?

Can crop circles also be square?

Why is quicksand called quicksand when it actually pulls you under veeeeeeery slowly?

How did the Dead Sea die?

If it's zero degrees outside and the TV weatherman warns it's going to be twice as cold tomorrow, what will the temperature be?

Why is it that night falls but day breaks?

When day breaks, who fixes it?

When would happen if night fell and the earth wasn't there to catch it?

Where does the white go when snow melts?

Why are some areas known as the 'downs' when they are actually quite hilly? Or are you only meant to go one way?

Why are violets blue, not violet?

Why aren't blueberries blue?

Can you cry underwater?

If a man in a forest says something and there is no woman around to hear him, is he still wrong?

Why do we use the phrase 'after dark' when, in truth, it's after light?

Isn't "a day without sunshine" a night?

Where does the fire go when the fire goes out?

When something fades in the sunlight, where does all the colour go?

When does a large puddle become a pond and a pond become a lake?

Would the speed of lightning be even quicker if it didn't zigzag around so much?

When does it stop being partially cloudy and start being partially sunny?

How can you chop down a tree and then chop it up?

If you yell at your plants rather than talk to them, will they grow up troubled and insecure?

How can the weather be as hot as Hell one day and as cold as Hell another?

Why is it that when the stars are out, they are visible, but when the lights are out, they are invisible?

Do Nordic meteorologists drink in isobars?

Has anyone ever actually seen it rain cats and dogs?

Why do the moons of all the other planets in our solar system have grandiose names like 'Titan', but the one in orbit around the earth is simply called the moon? Is this a very modest understatement, or actually a very pretentious one, as being *the* moon, rather than a moon?

Why does lighting a barbecue always make a gale-force wind blow?

If a tree fell onto a mime in the forest, would he make a sound?

What did we do before the Law of Gravity was passed?

If the universe is 'everything', yet scientists claim it is expanding, what can it possibly be expanding into?

If water spins clockwise when it drains in the northern hemisphere, and anti-clockwise when it drains in the southern hemisphere, what does it do at the equator?

Why is it that, when things get wet, they get darker, even though water is clear?

If we found conclusive proof of intelligent life on other planets, how would this affect the Miss Universe pageant?

If there was a 50mph wind blowing towards you, and you drove your car at precisely 50mph, would you feel the wind at all?

If you're caught between a rock and a hard place, does that suggest that the rock is soft?

If someone looked at the planet Earth from a distance, would it look as if some aircraft were flying upside down?

Why is it called eggplant when there is no egg in it?

Why is it called black light when it's really purple?

Why is our planet not called Ocean, rather than Earth, since more than three-quarters of it are covered in water?

If planets are in the sky, aren't we in the sky, too?

How is it that a trees are made of a wood, yet a wood is made of trees?

If space is a vacuum, who changes the bags?

Why do trees grow straight up when growing on the side of a steeply-sloped mountain?

Where does the flame of a candle go when you blow it out?

Where does the dark go when you switch on the light?

What's at the other end of a rainbow?

When it rains, the sky is completely covered in clouds, so how does the rain get through?

If the speed of movement is slower than the speed of light, how fast is a moving light?

If a tree falls in the forest and there is no one around to see it, do the other trees make fun of it?

If you were travelling at the speed of sound and you turned on the radio in your car, would you be able to hear it?

When lightning strikes the ocean, why don't all the fish die?

If you saw a heat wave, would you wave back?

Do you realise how many holes there could be if people would just take the time to take the dirt out of them?

If Mars has earthquakes, are they called marsquakes?

If you blew a bubble in space, would it pop?

Why are all the planets spherical?

Can you stare off into space when you're *in* space?

Why are dandelions considered to be weeds while daisies are considered to be flowers?

Where do all the daylight saving hours go?

What shape is the sky?

If you start digging a hole in the South Pole, are you digging down or up?

Is there a certain temperature at which it stops being qualified as cold? At what temperature does it officially qualify as hot?

If you took a compass into outer space, would it still point to magnetic north? Is there still a north, south, east and west in space?

Can you blow up a balloon under water?

If lava melts rock, why doesn't lava melt the volcano it comes out of?

Do bubbles freeze in winter?

Occupational Hazards

Do hairdressers get any fringe benefits?

Why aren't all financial advisors stinking rich, if they are any good at their jobs?

If a shop is open 24-hours a day, 365-days of the year, why does it have locks on the doors?

Why do kamikaze pilots wear safety helmets?

If an antique shop had a sale, would the prices go up?

Do bank managers laugh all the way to the office, to work or to somewhere else?

Do retired lumberjacks get the chop?

Do refuse collectors receive special training or are they expected to pick it up as they go along?

If talk is cheap, how do you explain lawyers?

Why is the man who invests all our money and apparently has your financial welfare at heart known as a broker?

If money doesn't grow on trees, why do banks have branches?

Why do banks charge you an "insufficient funds" fee, when they already know that you don't have the money to pay it?

Do taxidermists really know their stuff?

Do lollipop ladies make you cross?

Does the person who inventories sheep often fall asleep on the job?

When electricians get angry, do they blow a fuse?

Do cartographers have their ups and downs? Or is a cartographer someone who captures images of vehicles?

When would-be archaeologists are studying at university, do they live in student digs? When they make it known that they aim to pursue a future in archaeology, does their career advise warn them that their life will be in ruins?

If sign-writers go on strike, are their picket-line placards and banners all blank?

Can a postman get the sack on his first day?

Does a postman deliver his own letters? Does he take them directly home from the sorting office or does he deliver them while out on a round?

How does an estate agency sell its office without causing confusion?

When filling out HR/personnel forms, in the section headed "in case of emergency, please contact...", why don't people write "the ambulance service" or "a doctor" rather than putting down the name of a family member who would, more often than not, be useless in an emergency.

If a clown is sacked for looking miserable, would he have a case for funfair dismissal?

Do pilots take crash courses?

Why do we never hear about all the gruntled employees?

Is there any point advising a nightshift worker to "not quit the day job?"

If the government found a way to solve the unemployment problem and find a job for everyone, what would happen to the people who work in the job centres?

How does a shelf salesman stop his store from looking empty?

If FedEx and UPS were to merge, would they call the new company "FedUp?"

Why do you need to make an appointment to see a psychic? Surely they should know that you are coming? Similarly, if you telephoned a psychic helpline and they asked you your name, would you hang up, suspecting it's a scam? If they were truly psychic, of course, surely you wouldn't need to call them, they could call you first, wouldn't they? And if psychics were truly any good, why don't you ever see newspaper headlines about them winning the Lotto?

Do pediatricians play miniature golf?

When computer programmers die, do they click the bucket?

If a professional piano player is known as a pianist, why isn't a Grand Prix driver referred to as a racist?

Now that it has become so big, wouldn't it be more accurate to call Microsoft Macrosoft?

Do cemetery workers prefer the graveyard shift?

Why do bills travel through the post at twice the speed of cheques?

If you don't pay an exorcist for their services, will you get repossessed?

Why do scientists call what they do 're-search' when, in fact, they are looking for something new?

If a bus station is where the bus stops, and a train station is where the train stops, why is my position in the office called a work station?

Why is the army referred to as the 'infantry' when you've got to be aged over 18 before you can get in?

If Pizza Express was to open a restaurant next to a branch of the optician's chain Vision Express, would they accidentally get some of their neighours' customers?

If work is so terrific, why do employers have to pay you do to it?

What do they use to package up bubble-wrap in? Do they wrap it in Styrofoam, and then package Styrofoam in bubble-wrap?

How do they get the air inside the bubbles in bubble-wrap?

When you see a door in an office block or warehouse that says "this door is alarmed", don't you ever wonder about what caused its state of anxiety?

Do scarecrows ever get commended for being outstanding in their field?

If a cemetery suddenly increased its fees, could the rises be blamed on the cost of living?

Have former civil lawyers (a potential contradiction in terms in itself) been distorted?

Do retired bankers become disinterested?

Have former locomotive drivers become derailed?

How does a shepherd account for every sheep in his flock without falling asleep in the process?

Do former cowboys become de-ranged?

Do retired dry-cleaners become depressed?

Why does closing up a shop and closing down a shop have the same effect, namely that you can't buy anything from that shop?

If a magician loses his box of tricks, has he become disillusioned? Or is this what happens if you are banished from the Magic Circle?

Can a magician make something vanish into thick air, or is that pushing his powers just a little too much?

If a dentist calls what he does a 'practice', but then says he is going to take out a teeth for real, does he then say that, although it is a dental practice, what he is about to do is *not* a drill?

Why is it that, during a debate or business meeting, one person will respond to a point made by someone else by commenting: "I hear what you say…" when it's perfectly obvious that they have done, otherwise they would not be responding. In a lengthy discussion, it is then quite common for someone else to say "everything I wanted to say has already been said, but I just want to say…" and they then go on to say what has already been said, all over again. Why do people do that?

Did they have antique shops in the olden days (or were such outlets branded as 'nearly new'?)

Can't anybody who is an employee of any company walk through a door which says "staff only"? Wouldn't it make more sense to say "only for employees of this business"?

Do retired mathematicians become dysfunctional?

Have ex-punsters been expunged?

Does the Postmaster General need a stamp of approval?

How is it that you fill in a form by filling it out?

Why do they call the clock where workers punch their time cards a "time clock"? Aren't ALL clocks time clocks?

Do dentists go to other dentists for treatment, or do they do it themselves?

Why do shops have signs on the doors saying "guide dogs only" when guide dogs can't read?

Why do cobblers always cut keys?

Why do supermarkets have so many checkout lines when they only keep three or four open at a time?

If a teacher was ordered to teach a younger year group than they had been teaching before, would they consider themselves to be degraded?

Does a model who gets fired in favour of a younger, prettier model consider herself to be deposed?

If the restaurant chain Hooters started operating a door-to-door service, would it be named Knockers?

When a store has double doors, why do they only let you use one of them?

If you work in a hospital, is it OK to call in sick?

If you work for The Samaritans and you phoned in sick one morning, would your boss talk you out of it?

If the postal service has machines that can sort mail by the thousands per minute, why do they still rely on staff on bikes to deliver the letters?

People's Peculiarities

Why do we say "I'm going to call it a day" before going to bed at night time?

Why are old ladies always described as 'little'? Where are all the large ones?

Why are there never any guilty bystanders?

If a man is engaged several times, but never gets married, are his former fiancé's referred to as near Mrs?

Do bleached-blondes pretend to have more fun?

If a dog is man's best friend, but diamonds are a girl's best friend, you work out who gets the better deal!

Do infants enjoy infancy as much as many adults enjoy adultery?

How do you know you can't fool all of the people all of the time?

How can people tell you if they are truly speechless?

If an Earl is awarded an OBE, does he become an Earlobe?

If people with one arm go to get their nails done, do they pay half-price?

Would you give your right arm to be ambidextrous?

Why do people talk about 'girlie' things but never mention 'boyie' things?

If a dear child swears, does their mother wash their hands in soap and water? And is it considered rude for a deaf person to sign while their mouth is full?

Does a truly indecisive person know that they're indecisive, because if they're that sure…

If you can have a worst nightmare, does it naturally follow that you can have a best one?

If you have a disturbing dream during the day, why isn't it called a daymare? You can, after all, day dream!

Can you day dream at night?

Why can't we tickle ourselves?

Can a short person talk down to someone who is taller than them?

If a bald person works as a chef in a restaurant, does he still have to wear a hairnet?

If one identical twin takes out a patent on his face, does the other twin have to spend his entire life walking around in disguise, for fear of being sued for copyright?

If someone has a mid-life crisis while playing hide and seek, does he automatically lose because he can't find himself?

If you are a kleptomaniac, is there something you can take for it?

If boy scouts are forever doing good turns, don't they get dizzy?

If you take an Oriental person to the fairground and put him on a really fast, spinning, ride, does he become disorientated?

When blind people go on a blind date, what do they call it?

Why is it that writers write but fingers don't fing, grocers don't groce and hammers don't ham?

Is it true that six fifths of the population have trouble with fractions?

Is it true that there are only three types of people in the world; those who can count, and those who can't?

If you try to fail and succeed, what have you done?

If you are old enough to know better, are you too old to do it?

Does he who laughs last not actually laugh longest but, in truth, think slowest?

If quitters never win, and winners never quit, what was the thinking behind the phrase "quit while you are ahead"?

Would an astronaut's party have any atmosphere?

How many people does it take to change a searchlight bulb?

Who does suffer fools gladly?

Why does anyone with a photographic memory own a camera?

How do people with a bad memory always remember that they have a bad memory, yet don't remember much else?

If you are not a complete idiot, which bits are usually missing?

Are people more violently opposed to fur, rather than leather, because it's easier to harass rich women than motorcycle gangs?

Who was the real McCoy?

How did the first person to count from one-to-ten know that he was right?

How do you write zero in Roman numerals?

Is a 'ghetto blaster' a terrorist in a slum neighbourhood?

If masochists like to torture themselves, wouldn't they do it best by not torturing themselves, in which case, aren't most of us masochists?

How can you hear yourself think?

If you hate people who are prejudiced, are you a hypocrite?

How do you know if you never forget a face?

If a silly or unintelligent man can be branded 'gormless', is his intellectual opposite referred to as being 'gorm'?

If an incompetent person is 'inept', is a competent person 'ept'?

Do people ever reach the middle of their tether and, if so, are they perfectly content?

Surely if a woman is taking the, potentially lifelong, step of committing herself to marriage, she'd have a better chance of it working out if she married the 'best' man?

What is the female equivalent of a 'sugar daddy' and 'toy boy'?

How do you know *which* cheek is the 'other' one?

Does a flirtatious under-achiever sleep their way to the middle?

Can someone who is stone-cold sober be described as being ebriated?

Why do people point to their wrist when they are asking someone for the time, but never to their nether-regions when asking for the location of the nearest bathroom?

Why do people without a watch always instinctively look at their wrist when you ask them what time it is?

Why is it that so many people say "can you talk" when someone has just answered the phone to them and have already said "hello"?

Why is it that when a man talks dirty to a woman, it is regarded as sexual harassment, but when a woman talks dirty to a man, it is £4.50 per minute?

If a love-struck couple decided to tie the knot in a portable toilet, would this be considered a marriage of convenience?

Why do people say "it's always in the last place you look?" Of course it is, because once you've found it, surely you'll stop looking!

Why aren't there any Father-in-Law jokes?

If a chronic, compulsive, liar tells you that he is a chronic, compulsive, liar, should you believe him or not?

Why are people so afraid of falling, when it's actually reaching the ground that kills them?

If your best friend works for the Psychic Friends Network, is there ever any point in trying to arrange a surprise party for him?

If light travels faster than sound, does that explain why some people appear to be quite bright until you hear them speak?

Can blind people see their dreams?

How can you be alone with somebody?

If you had a clone, and it tried to murder you, would this be regarded as a suicide attempt?

Do jilted farmers receive John Deere letters?

Why do people say "heads up" when, in actual fact, they are suggesting that the best thing you can do with some urgency is to duck?

How to you respond to someone who incorrectly suggests that you are in denial?

If your name was Anonymous, would you get credit for everything that nobody wanted credit for?

Why do we say we feel blue when we are depressed? And what colour does a Smurf turn when it is depressed?

Why do we feel like we've got the weight of the world on our shoulders, but when we come to talk about it, we have to get it off our chest?

If you accuse someone of being judgmental, aren't you judging them?

Why do they call it being 'head over heels' in love, when our heads are commonly over our heels, so this circumstance is not anything remotely out of the ordinary or extra special?

If you tell some untruths, why is it described as telling porkies?

Can someone named Nick also have a nickname, of was that it?

If two identical twin brothers married two identical twin sisters, would they be able to tell their children apart?

What would happen if you mooned a werewolf?

Are attractive Eskimo girls considered to be 'hot'?

If someone says "you're not yourself today", would an appropriate reply be "if that's the case, why are you telling me?"

Is it true that there are two theories about arguing with women, but neither of them work?

Do Siamese twins pay for one ticket or two when they go to the movies or concerts, or book travel tickets?

If you're born at exactly midnight, which of the days does your birthday fall on, or is it both? (In which case, are you going to age twice as quickly as everyone else?)

If we say "bye-bye", why don't we say "hi-hi?"

Can a dyslexic blind person still read Braille?

Why does everyone speak different languages and have different accents if we all originally came from the same place?

If someone can't see, they are blind; if they can't hear, they are deaf; if they can't speak, they are dumb; what do you call someone who can't smell?

Is the fear of flying groundless?

Why do people say "you scared the living daylights out of me" when daylight is not living?

Why is it that when people are asked "what one thing would you bring with you to a desert island?" they struggle to think of a suitable answer and very, very, rarely say "a boat"?

When a genie appears and offers someone three wishes, why isn't the first thing they say "I wish you would grant me an infinite number of wishes?"

Why do people keep old raffle tickets in their wallets or purses when they know the draw was months ago and they clearly haven't won?

What do people expect you to say when you ask "can I ask you a question?" Even if you say no, you are contradicting yourself by answering a question!

If you're filling in a form, and it asks you to specify you hair colour, what do you write if you are as bald as a cue ball?

If something goes without saying, why do people then still go on to say it?

Why do you forget what you were looking for as soon as you leave the room?

If you can mix two primary colours of paint to make all the other colours, why do manufactures both to make other colours of paint?

Why is a drunk unintelligible to anyone sober, but two drunks can have an in-depth discussion about nuclear physics?

If there are two sides to every argument, what happens when the parties in a ménage-a-trois fall out?

If Americans throw rice at weddings, do Oriental people throw hamburgers?

How do environmentalists get to all the 'green' rallies and conventions that they attend? They can't possibly walk or cycle to all of them, surely?

Can cross-eyed teachers control their pupils?

Why is there always "one in every crowd"? If you took all the ones in every crowd out, and put them into a crowd of their own, would there still be one in that crowd?

Why do people say "I'm all at sixes and sevens?" What exactly does this mean, and is being at sixes or sevens better, or rose, than being at fours and fives, and eights and nines?

When one person says to another, "don't have a cow", what do two cows say to each other, "don't have a person?"

Is a man full of wonder a wonderful man?

Why do people who know the least know it the loudest?

Could it be that all those Halloween trick or treaters who wear white sheets aren't going out as ghosts, but as mattresses?

When two men marry each other, do they go to the same bachelor party?

Do Jewish vampires avoid crosses or Stars of David?

Why do parents spend all year teaching their children not to take sweets from strangers, and then send them out trick or treating on Halloween?

Why is it that if someone yells 'duck', they are helping you but if they yell 'chicken', they are insulting you?

Why are people so scared of mice which are so much smaller than them, yet are happy to pose for photos with Mickey Mouse at Disneyland, who is often taller than them?

Do Chinese people get English phrases and sayings tattooed onto their bodies?

Do stuttering people stutter when they're thinking to themselves?
If someone in the US had both legs amputated, would they have to change their height and weight on their drivers' licence?

Do people who use sign language see little hands in their head when they think about what somebody said, or do they hear the words in their head?

Is someone still described as 'late' if they die young?

Why does every Abraham Lincoln impersonator sound the same, even though there are no known audio recordings of the man himself?

How is it that people tell you to stay a kid for as long as you can, yet the moment you do anything childish or immature, they tell you to grow up?

Why are elderly people commonly called 'old people', but children are never called 'new people'?

When a 'grown-up', as opposed to a 'kid', is abducted and taken hostage, why isn't it referred to as an adultnapping?

Why is it that people duck in the rain? Do they really think that the rain won't hit them if they crouch down?

Is an alcoholic just a drunk with a phobia about hangovers?

How is it that, when people start to sing, they automatically sing in a higher voice than their talking voice?

Can someone have their head in the clouds and be down to earth at the same time?

Do nudists have pin-ups of people with clothes on? Do nudist camps stop operating during colder months; are they clothed for winter?

Why is it that when we're in the supermarket and someone rams our ankle with a shopping trolley, and apologises, we say, "it's all right" when our inner voice is screaming "that bloody hurt, you idiot!"

If marriage means you fell in love, does divorce mean you climbed out?

Why do people say "PIN number", when the full meaning of that phrase would be "Personal Identification Number Number"?

Why do people call it an ATM machine, which is actually saying "Automated Teller Machine Machine"?

Why is it that when we laugh in the classroom, the teacher asks if you find something funny, when it's quite clear that we do?

When a boy is named after his father, he is often called 'Junior' but what do you call a girl who is named after her mother?

If a missing person sees their picture on a poster that offers a reward for information concerning their whereabouts, would they claim the reward if they made themselves known to the authorities?

When people say "I'm so tired, it's not even funny", or "my head hurts so much, it's not even funny", why would it be particularly amusing in the first place?

Why do bullies ask "what's your problem?" when they've clearly got no genuine interest in solving it?

People say you should always give 100 percent in everything you do; but surely that doesn't apply to donating blood, does it?

Religious (dis)Beliefs

Why do so many images of Adam and Eve show them with navels?

On his birthday, did Jesus get a Christmas present, too?

What happened to all the gold brought by the three wise men? Mary and Joseph could probably have bought the entire Inn with all that gold, let alone afford one room, so they would not have to have spent the night in a smelly stable.

If the son of God went on to produce a variety of dairy products, would his shop be called Cheeses of Nazareth?

If you stole all the joss sticks from a Buddhist monastery, would they be incensed?

If priests wear dog collars, do dogs wear priest collars?

If Noah had two of everything in the ark, how did he manage with woodworm and woodpeckers? Why did ducks need to seek refuge in the ark? Were bees kept in archives?

Why didn't Noah swat the two mosquitoes?

Do Muslims have Christian names?

Can atheists get insurance for acts of God?

Is atheism a non-prophet organisation?

If you're in Hell, and you get really mad with someone, where do you tell them to go?

Does God believe that there are athiests?

To make holy water do you boil the hell out of ordinary water?

Does a lightning rod on top of a church indicate a lack of faith?

If God created everyone in his own image, why do peoples of the world all look so very different?

Was Joseph's surname 'Christ' too?

If God dropped acid, would he see people?

If hot air rises, and Hell is supposed to be *that* hot, surely the air would rise and Hell would actually be quite chilly!

If God sneezed, what would you say?

Why is it that when we talk to God, we are praying, but when we suggest that God talks to us, we locked in the loony bin?

If God created everything, and He knows everything ahead of time, why did he create Satan?

Why is the angel of death called an angel if all it does is bring pain and suffering?

Once you're in Heaven, assuming you make it, are you stuck wearing the same clothes you were buried in for all of eternity?

If it is true that we are here to help others, then what are the others here for?

If a funeral procession took place at night, do people drive with their lights off?

Why are there no stories in the Bible about Jesus' teenage years?

What was the best-selling book before the Bible?

Now that churches have female clergy, should congregations start singing Hyrs as well as Hymns and, in these times of political correctness and equality, should prayers end with the word "Aperson"?

Do coffins have lifetime guarantees?

Do mass murderers only kill in church?

If a priest decided to get married, would he hire another priest or would he conduct the wedding himself?

When the Pope goes to the bathroom, is the result considered to be a holy crap?

If Sunday is supposed to be a holy day of rest, why do people have to get up so early to get to church?

Can someone give up lent for lent?

If the day before December 25 is called Christmas Eve, shouldn't the day after be called Christmas Adam?

Why are there, apparently, "12 days of Christmas" when Christmas Day is clearly 25 December, one single day?

Sport and Pastime Posers

Is it more than a coincidence that there is a 'p' in swimming pool?

Is PPI something that you only get in swimming pools while a school party is in?

In water polo, where are the horses?

Can fat people go skinny dipping? If so, shouldn't it be called something a little more appropriate, like 'chunky dunking'?

Do dwarves surf on microwaves?

What if the hokey cokey really IS what it's all about?

Why do we play in recitals but recite in plays?

Can you buy an entire chess set in a pawn shop, or just one type of piece?

If you jog backwards, do you gain weight?

What happens if you go on a survival course but you don't pass?

Do Chinese children who are learning to play the piano get taught how to play a tune called Knifes and Forks?

What is the point of a team being in a league of its own? Who would they play against?

How can a team be second to none? Surely, that would actually make you first?

If it's the tourist season, does that mean that it's legal to shoot them?

Why does 'love' mean zero in tennis?

Why don't tennis scores go 1, 2, 3, rather than 15, 30 and 40?

Is Disneyland a giant people trap operated by a large mouse?

How many musicians are in a rubber band?

Why do bars advertise performances from 'live' bands? Surely a dead band would not be likely to encourage anyone to get up and dance?

If a book is listed as being available from all good bookshops, what do all the bad bookshops sell?

Do newly-published books about poltergeists fly off the shelves?

If you are told not to judge a book by its cover, why don't they simply put different covers on books?

If one synchronised swimmer had a heart attack and drowned in the middle of a performance, what would happen to the other swimmers?

How can one person claim to be a synchronised swimmer? Who does he/she synchronise with?

If the game of rugby was invented in a south London school, would it be known as Tooting Secondary Modern, instead?

What do you call a male ballerina?

Why are softballs so hard?

Do exceptional dancers have two right feet?

Is an unsociable foxtrot a dance in which everyone is treading on each other's toes on purpose?

Is camping loitering within tent?

Why is a boxing 'ring' square?

When they televise snow sports, why do programme makers insist on insulting the intelligence of viewers by emphasising that the event is 'downhill skiing', when most people would reasonably be expected to conclude that it's highly likely that nobody ever won a gold medal by skiing up a mountain?

If athletes contest that marathons may be superior to sprints, could their attitude be described as being race-ist?

Where do forest rangers go to get away from it all?

Does an artist with asthma find it difficult to draw breath?

If a book about failure doesn't sell a single copy, is this regarded as a success?

Why are the viewing areas at all-seater football stadia still referred to as stands?

Why don't poor sports teams wear their shirts back to front to make it look as if they are attacking?

Is 'drag racing' a competition to be the first person to get from the start to the finish while wearing clothing usually associated with the opposite gender?

How is it possible to have a "greatest album in the world ever…volume three"?

Is recycling a return journey on a bicycle?

Are part-time big band leaders semi-conductors?

Why is baseball's World Series so called, when it's only played in the USA and Canada?

Why is American Football called football when they barely use their feet at all?

Did the early settlers ever go away on camping trips?

If a jogger runs faster than the speed of sound, will they still be able to hear their Walkman?

Do racing car drivers need their licence when they get behind the wheel at a race track?

Why is a Running Back called a Running Back when he spends most of his time running forwards?

Why do people never say "it's only a game" when they're winning?

If, in a baseball game, the batter hits a ball in such a way that it splits right down the middle, with one half flying out of the park but the other half being caught, what is the final ruling?

Why do people think that swaying their arm back and forth will significantly change the direction of a bowling ball?

If swimming is supposed to be so good for you, why are whales the shape they are?

Why do ballet dancers always dance on their tiptoes? Wouldn't it make more sense to simply hire dancers who are naturally taller?

Do dancers choose ballet as their preferred discipline after putting tu and tu together?

Why is it that if we skate on thin ice, we could end up in *hot* water?

What's the difference between a novel and a book?

How can chess be considered a sport?

If conjoined twins participate in sports, do they count as one player or two?

Why is it that it's good to score under par in golf, but it's bad to be under par in just about everything else?

Structurally (un)Sound

If you have a three-storey house and you are on the second floor, are you upstairs and downstairs at the same time?

Why are they called steps outside but stairs inside?

If you have detached and semi-detached homes, why are homes in the middle of a row called terraced rather than attached?

Are French homes made out of Plaster of Paris?

Why are some smaller residential units called apartments when they are all stuck together?

Why are structures called buildings, which suggests a work in progress? Shouldn't completed structures be called builts?

Why do tourists go to the top of very tall buildings, often paying for the privilege, only to then pay to use telescopes to see what's on the ground?

Does Bill Gates' house have windows and a hard drive?

Can you get cornered in a round room?

Why are toilets at petrol stations so often locked? Are they afraid that there's a danger of someone sneaking in and cleaning them?

Why is a women's prison called a penal colony?

Why do people tell you not to stand in front of an emergency exit when, if there was an emergency, surely you would run through it?

Do they have girl's bathrooms in gay bars?

Do stairs go up or down?

Technology Traumas

Why is a single old television referred to as a set?

Why do you press harder on the buttons of a remote control when you know that the battery is dead?

Why do people repeatedly jab at the button to summon a lift when you know that it won't make the elevator arrive any quicker?

Why is the third hand on a watch called the second hand?

Why do people say that their alarms are going off when they have just turned on?

When Alexander Graham Bell first invented the telephone, who did he call?

Is it OK to use AM radio after midday?

When they first invented the clock, how did they know what time to set it to?

If a sundial was used to tell the time during sunlight, how did people used to tell the time at night? And what happens when you are supposed to put the clocks forward and back an hour?

If people were not meant to indulge in midnight snacks, why do the manufacturers include lights inside refrigerators?

Why isn't there a light in the freezer, like there is in a fridge? Is this because it would take too long for something to thaw out for a midnight feast?

Why is there a 'd' in 'fridge' but not in refrigerator?

Has anyone tried to invent a solar-powered flashlight?

Why does the ear-piercing low battery warning on a smoke alarm always start sounding at 3am, and not a far more sociable hour?

How do I set my laser printer to stun?

If you sneezed onto a computer, would it get a virus?

Is a four-ply tissue anti-virus soft-wear?

Why is it that in order to stop Windows on a computer, you have to go to the Start button?

Why are there often Braille dots on the keypad of a drive-up cashpoint machine?

If a streetlight lights up a street, and a fog light lights up fog, why would anyone in their right mind want a spotlight?

If you are reviewing something and you say that it "really sucks", this usually means it is not remotely efficient/effective/good; what if you were reviewing a vacuum cleaner?

Who is 'General Failure' and why does he try to read other people's hard drives?

Why does the telephone start ringing as soon as you sit on the toilet or get into the shower, but stop as soon as you pick it up?

If an escalator breaks down, does it simply become stairs?

Why isn't the 'caps lock' button on computer keyboards capitalised?

Why don't radio show presenters shout out over the airwaves, "Alexa, ensure that the radio is tuned only to this station all day long"?

Why do they call it an elevator when it takes you down?

If two of the biggest and best-known social media channels were to merge, would the new entity be known as TwitFace?

Why are there no pictures of 'no flash photography' signs?

If the Energizer Bunny attacked someone, would it be charged with battery?

On a telephone, why does 'ABC' start on the number 2 and not on the number 1?

Why do radio operators say "niner" instead of "nine"?

Why do the numbers on a telephone go one way and the numbers on a calculator go the other?

Why is an electrical outlet called an outlet when you plug things into it? Surely it should be called an inlet?

Why is there an eject button on some remote controls, when you still have to get up to retrieve the CD/DVD/Bluray disc from the player?

How do the cell phone companies choose your cell phone number and will they one day run out of numbers to issue?

Why do people who are using touch-tone phones still say that they are dialling a number?

If mirrors need light to work, what happens if you put night vision goggles on in the dark and then look at a mirror?

Why is the '0' on a phone after the '1' and not before it?

Why aren't there any B batteries?

Travel and Transport Tribulations

Why do we travel on planes, trains, boats and buses, but *in* cars?

Do flying fish ever lose their luggage?

If flying is so safe, why is the airport call a terminal?

How far west can you go before you're heading east?

If you got into a taxi and insisted that he drive backwards, would the driver end up owing you money?

Is it legal to drive down a road in reverse, as long as you are going in the same direction as the main flow of traffic?

How can a leaf gently fall from a tree and wedge itself so tightly under your windscreen wiper that even a 70mph wind can't dislodge it?

Why are level crossings so uneven and bumpy?

Why is a slip road only slippery when there's ice on the road? Shouldn't it be called a non-slip road at other times?

Why do some airlines promote their flights as non-stop? This means they would never land anywhere, which means you will never get to where you want to get; what's more, at some point, they will run out of fuel and fall out of the sky.

If a lorry carrying a container full of budgies goes over a bump and all the budgies fly off their perches, does the lorry weigh less?

If a lorry carrying many crates of nasal spray crashes and spills its load all over the carriageway, is it true that there will be no congestion for up to eight hours?

If a lorry laden with snooker equipment was to crash and shed its load, having slipped on a bridge, will the cues stretch back for miles and the driver be put under a rest?

Why is it that anyone who drives slower than you is an idiot and anyone who drives faster than you is a maniac?

Why is the name 'rush hour' given to a time when traffic is the slowest on the roads?

Is it absolutely necessary to have a driver in an automatic car?

Why do they put frosted glass on the windows of toilets in aircraft?

Why are bus shelters called bus shelters, when you can't fit even a small bus under them?

Why are there flotation devices under the seats in an aircraft? Would not a parachute under each seat be a tad more useful?

Why do the signs that say 'Slow Children' include an image of a running child?

Why is it that transporting something by car is called a shipment but when doing it by ship, it's called cargo?

Why are all makes of car allowed to use Mini roundabouts?

If you are driving in a car with the headlights on, and you somehow manage to travel faster than the speed of light, will you still be able to see where you are going?

When two aircraft almost collide, why do they call it a near miss? They did not nearly miss each other, they nearly hit each other. It should be called a near hit.

Why are explosive projectiles called missiles? Wouldn't hittiles be a more accurate term?

If you go to a train station and ask to buy a return ticket, why does the cashier ask "where to?" when the obvious answer is "back here?"

If a stealth bomber crashes in a forest, does it make a sound?

What would Geronimo shout if he jumped out of a plane?

Is a hot car 'cool', or a cool car 'hot'?

Do airport security guards have to go through airport security when they arrive at work each day?

Why do people bother to book flights with Virgin Airways, entrusting their travel plans to someone who, by definition, doesn't go all the way?

Why do we park in a drive but we are not allowed to drive in a park?

If an ice cream van was involved in a road traffic collision, would the driver suffer from whippylash and crushed nuts? (Would there be a flakey suggestion that he had tried to top himself? Maybe had had a meltdown. Presumably the road would be coned off and people would be told they could not drive that wafer long. Alternatively, could it be an insurance scam in a bid to claim some lolly, perhaps hundreds of thousands, as a result of which he could have his assets frozen, be sentenced to twenty licks and a spell in the cooler?)

Why do 'tug' boats push barges?

If most car accidents happen within five miles of home, why doesn't everyone move ten miles away?

Is the reason that it can be difficult to understand the words of a long-distance lorry driver when he is sitting in his cab because he happens to be inarticulate(d)?

Where does the airbag cover on a car's steering wheel go when the bag is deployed? Given how quickly an airbag inflates, is it possible that the cover springs out so quickly that it hits you in the face?

Who tows the tow trucks when they break down?

If you are on a plane travelling at the speed of sound, and you walked from the back to the front, are you walking faster than the speed of sound?

If you took a short flight from one time zone into another, but didn't adjust your watch, is it possible to land before you took off, and in that case, would you need to wait at the airport for time to catch up with itself before you could continue with the rest of your journey?

How did the headless horseman know where he was going?

Can you walk "down the road" even if the road goes up hill?

Why is it then when you are driving around and looking for an address, you turn down the volume on the radio?

How can Hawaii have interstate highways?

Can you prong your car, if there is a fork in the road?

Why do Americans call the cheapest class of travel and planes and trains 'coach'?

Why is it acceptable to use a driver's licence as proof of identity when buying alcohol, when it's illegal to drink and drive?

Because it IS illegal – and dangerous – to drive while under the influence of alcohol, why do so many bars have car parks?

How fast do you have to travel to keep up with the sun so that you are never in darkness?

Would it be possible for a solar car to travel faster than the speed of light?

If a transport truck laden with cars is involved in a road accident, does it significantly increase the number of cars in the pile-up?

Why do so many cars have speedometers that go up to at least 130mph when you can't legally drive that fast on any road?

Why is there always someone driving right behind you in the quietest country lane?

Why are there 'yield' or 'stop/give way' signs in front of train tracks? Does anyone really think that they have the right of way over a train?

When a car is on a TV advertisement and it's moving forward, why to the wheels look like they're turning backwards?

Why are submarines fitted with screen doors?

Do temporary traffic lights ever get to hold down a permanent position?

Why are American drivers charged a toll on freeways?

Why is it that car keys are the only keys with teeth on both sides?

How is it that we put a man on the moon before we figured out it would be a good idea to put wheels on luggage?

Why do people say they go "back and forth" to town; surely you must really go forth before you can go back?

Why do they call steam rollers steam rollers? They don't produce, get rid of or have anything to do with steam, or the rolling out of steam?

How many parking spaces do you need in order to have a parking lot? Presumably, it's quite a few.

What happens when you get onto a plane, and shout a happy "Hi" to your friend Jack at the other end?

If you see a car for sale at a dealership, and it has a balloon attached to it, does the balloon come with the car if you buy it?

What exactly is the 'Baby on Board' sign for in a car? Does it help anyone decide which car not to hit, in case of an accident?

If you don't believe the claim that the only reason an airplane has a propeller at the front is to keep the pilot cool, just watch how much he starts to sweat if it stops working.

Wordy Wise

Why does fat chance and slim chance mean the same thing?

Why do slow down and slow up mean the same thing?

Why is dyslexic such a difficult word to spell?

Why does flammable and inflammable mean the same thing?

Why doesn't 'onomatopoeia' sound like what it is?

Why is the word 'phonetic' not spelled the way it sounds?

Which cruel tormentor thought it would be a good idea to put an 's' in the word 'lisp'?

Why isn't the word 'palindrome' spelled the same backwards?

If you can't spell Armageddon, is it the end of the world?

Who decided on the order of the letters in the alphabet? Or was it all to do with that wretched song?

If you do not read many books, can you be considered "thinly read"?

Why is there only one word for thesaurus?

If you lost your thesaurus, would you be able to find the words to describe how you feel?

If a pronoun is used in place of a noun, can a proverb be used in place of a verb?

Why don't dictionaries have an index?

What's another word for synonym?

Why do 'overlook' and 'oversee' mean opposite things?

Can you be in two minds as to whether or not something is ambiguous?

If a picture is worth a thousand words, what is a picture of a thousand words worth?

If 'horrific' means to make horrible, does 'terrific' mean to make terrible?

Why is 'abbreviated' such a long word?

When the word 'number' is abbreviated, where does the 'o' come from?

Why don't the words 'tomb', 'comb' and 'bomb' rhyme with each other?

If 'mice' is the plural of 'mouse', does this explain why posh people who own a number of domestic dwellings refer to the term 'hice'?

If a food processor slices and dices food, what does a word processor do? (Perhaps this can account for the typo's created by auto-correct's seemingly random slicing and dicing!).

What is the point of silent letters?

Which letter is silent in the word 'scent'? Is it the 's' or the 'c'?

Why do we say "bye-bye", but not "hi-hi"?

Why does the word 'one' have a 'w' sound in it, despite there being no 'w' present, yet the word 'two' doesn't have a 'w' sound?

Why is the abbreviation for a pound in weight written is lb, when the word pound has neither an 'l' or a 'b' in it?

Why is hippotomonstrosesquippedaliophobia the name for the fear of long words? It means that it will cause people great distress to tell you the name of the condition that causes them great distress. Surely it would have been better to call it something much shorter like 'eek'?

If one man says "it was an uphill struggle" and another said "it all went downhill from there", how can they both be having troubles?

How can the saying "it's all downhill from here" mean both that it will be easy and that it's going to get worse?

If you can be overwhelmed and underwhelmed, can you also be whelmed?

If stamp collectors are philatelists, why don't you ever hear somebody walk into a Post Office and ask for a book of first-class philats?

If quizzes are quizzical, what does that make tests? (Presumably, a load of bollocks, in other words!)

Why do we say that something is "out of whack"? What exactly is a whack, and how easy is it to get out of it? Can the opposite feeling or circumstance be described as being "in whack"?

Why are a wise man and a wise guy opposites?

Why are there five syllables in the word 'monosyllabic'?

If the plural of tooth is teeth, why isn't the plural of booth beeth?

If the text within a document or publication is original, why is it commonly referred to as copy?

Why is so hard to remember how to spell the word mnemonic?

Why is it that when you sit up and sit down, the result is the same?

The letter 'W' is called 'double U' but wouldn't it be more accurate to call it "double V'?

Who taught the first teacher?

If teachers taught, why didn't preachers praught?

Is cheese the plural of choose?

If goose is singular and geese is plural, is the correct plural of moose meese?

If mice is the plural of mouse, is rice actually the plural of rouse, but rouse is rarely used since it's not often reference is made to a single grain?

If the plural of tooth is teeth, why isn't the plural of booth beeth?

What exactly do the "P's" and "Q's" mean when people tell you to mind them?

If a word was not spelled correctly in the dictionary, how would we ever know?

If Webster wrote the first dictionary, where did he get all the words from?

What's the point of reading between the lines?

Is there such a thing as a dictionary of 'made-up' words, called a fictionary? Is there a film reference book called a flicktionary?

When does the obvious become blatant?

If 'laughter' is actually pronounced 'lafter', shouldn't that make everybody's daughter 'dafter'?

Is it possible to be totally partial?

If inert is to be stationary, what is ert?

If pro is the opposite of con, is progress the opposite of Congress?

Is it possible to make another complete word out of the word 'anagram'?

If 'a few' means not many, and 'a lot' means a large quantity – ie, they are opposites – how is it that 'quite a few' and 'quite a lot' means the same thing?

Why is the word 'four' the only number word that has the same quantity of letters as its numerical value?

Why do all the days of the week end in 'y'?

Why does blow and suck mean the same thing when it comes to describing something that is crap?

Why are words typed up but written down?

Why does caregiver and caretaker mean the same thing?

How can 'to cleave' mean both to split apart/sever and to stick together?

What is the opposite of opposite?

Why do we pass over underpasses, and pass under overpasses?

Why don't we pronounce the year 2000 as 'twenty hundred', like 1900; why don't we pronounce the year 2007 as twenty o'seven?

Why don't we pronounced the number 11 as 'one-ty one'?

Why is there an 'L' in 'Noel'?

How is it that thaw and unthaw mean the same thing?

How can overtones and undertones be the same thing?

Who coined the phrase 'coined the phrase'?

Isn't it ironic that the word 'teacher' is an anagram of cheater?

Why is "Joey" considered to be short for "Joe", when Joey has more letters?

Why are the adjectives 'fast as' and 'slow as' often used in conjunction with hell? Is hell slow or fast or both or neither?

There is a rule of grammar which says: "I before E, except after C". If that is correct, does that mean that the word science is spelled wrong?

Why do you delete something on a computer, but erase something on paper?

Do witches run spell checkers?

Did you realise that if you replace 'W' with 'T' in What, Where and When, you get the answer to each of them?

Bonus Content

You lucky people! As if I've not already subjected you to enough torment and torture, I thought that, if Mission Imponderable was a DVD or Bluray, then it would be expected to include some bonus features. And since I couldn't find enough of each example of the following type of witty wordplay (I use the term advisedly), I thought it would make perfect 'additional content' to add insult to the inevitable injury I've already inflicted upon you all (they don't call me the Pun-isher for nothing, you know!).

So, here's just a few random 'funnies', (once again, I use the term advisedly) just to finish off:

Mixed metaphor day

Why not really push the boat out and enjoy a mixed metaphor day? And since proverbs are often metaphorical, you can use a bit of 'journalistic licence' to mix and match them.

Have a go; it's not rocket surgery you know. Or brain science, come to that.

After all, a bird in hand makes it difficult to blow your nose.

Don't let sleeping dogs bite the hand that feeds them.

Too many cooks are a crowd.

A stitch in time gathers no moss.

You've buttered your bread, now lie in it.

Marriages Made In Heaven

Not imponderable questions as such, but they are questions, so they kind of count:

If British TV presenter Tess Daly married the cartoon character Mr Tickle, would she become Tess Tickle?

If the band Dire Straits created some music with singer Chris Rea, would their partnership be called Dire Rea?

If singer Stevie Nicks married veteran actor William Shatner, would her new name be Stevie Shatner-Nicks, which sounds messy?

If actress Whoopee Goldberg had married actor Peter Cushing, would she have used the name Whoopee Cushing?

If pop star Beyonce had married former British tennis player-turned-TV presenter Andrew Castle, would she use the name Beyonce Castle?

Collective Nouns
Is the collective noun for a group of photographers a 'focus'?
Is the collective noun for a group of PR practitioners a 'spin'?
Is the collective noun for a group of noisy children a 'migraine'?
Any ideas for what you call a collection of collective nouns? (A nonsense, maybe?)

Walkie Talkies
What would happen if the person responsible for naming the walkie-talkie had been given a wider influence over our language? Would we be using the following terms as commonly as we use walkie-talkie?

Dogfish: Barky Sharky.
Anchor: Droppy Stoppy.
A cigar or cigarette: Smoky Chokey.
Gutter: Rainy Drainy.
Undercooked or overcooked chicken: Yucky Clucky.
Roadkill: Splatty Catty.
Incoherent elderly person: Mumbly Crumbly.
Bra: Boulder Holder; Breast Nest.
Forefinger: Pointy Jointy.
Dessert: Eatie Treatie.
Spoon: Soupy Scoopy.
Fork: Stabby Grabbie.
Viagra: Phony Boney.
Bumble Bees: Fuzzy Buzzy.

Pregnancy test: Maybe Baby.
Socks: Feetie Heatie.
Hippo: Floatie Bloatie.
Postman: Letter Getter.
Thongs: Peekie Cheekies.
Missiles: Zoomy Boomies.
Super-glue: Stickie Quickie.
Screwdrivers: Rightie Tighties.
Wigs: Hairy Wearies.
Porn mags and erotic novels: Nookie Bookies.
Allergies: Wheezy Sneezies.
Litter tray: Kitty Shitty.
Rumbly tum: Growly Bowel-y.
Diesel car: Fumey Vroomy.
Foghorn/loudhailer: Shouty Spouty.
Fast female runner: Sprinty Binty.
Diva: Fussy Hussey.
Gluttonous child: Hoggy Sproggy.
Diahorrea: Sloppy Ploppy.
Trainee chef: Rookie Cookie.
The face you make after eating very hot food: Burny Gurny.
Communal wine: Vicar Liquor.
Diet meal: Thinner Dinner.
A witch's preferred travel method: Zoomie Broomy.
Man flu: A Lotty Snotty.
A warm beach: Toastie Coasty.
A diminutive sorceress: Titchy Witchy.
A cantankerous old woman: Moanie Croanie.
A male comedian or clown: Jokey Blokey.
A deer which narrowly escapes being hit by a car: Lucky Bucky.
A traffic jam: Slowie Go-ie.
The action required to drain a sink: Tuggy Pluggy.
Nightmare: Screamy Dreamy.
Stamps: Lickie Stickie.
Defibrillator: Hearty Starty.

L - #0106 - 210721 - C0 - 210/148/8 - PB - DID3131193